AF338280

Photography For Children

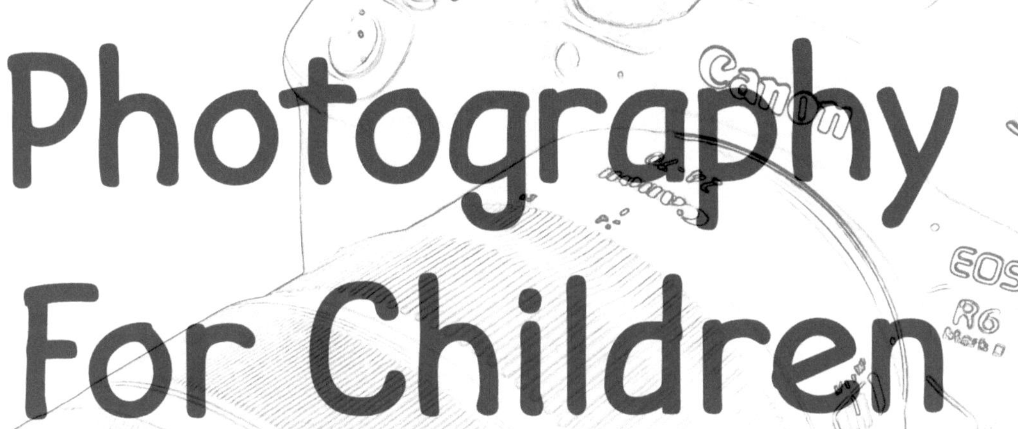

A young person's guide to taking pictures.

Sonja McGiboney

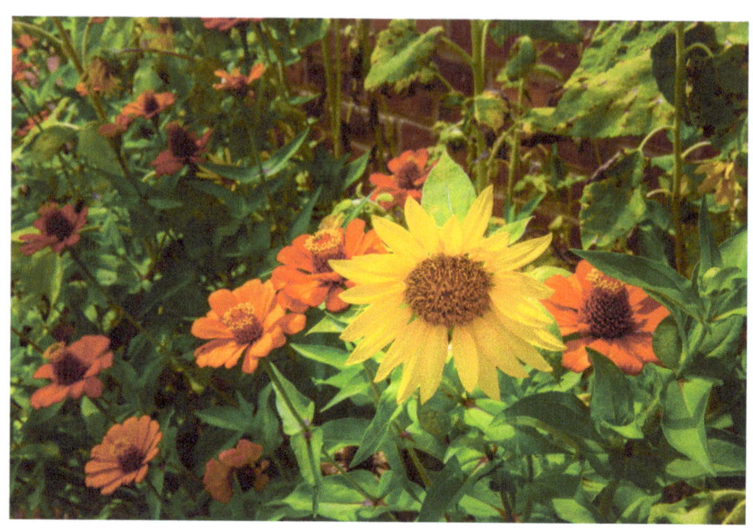

Photos capture color.

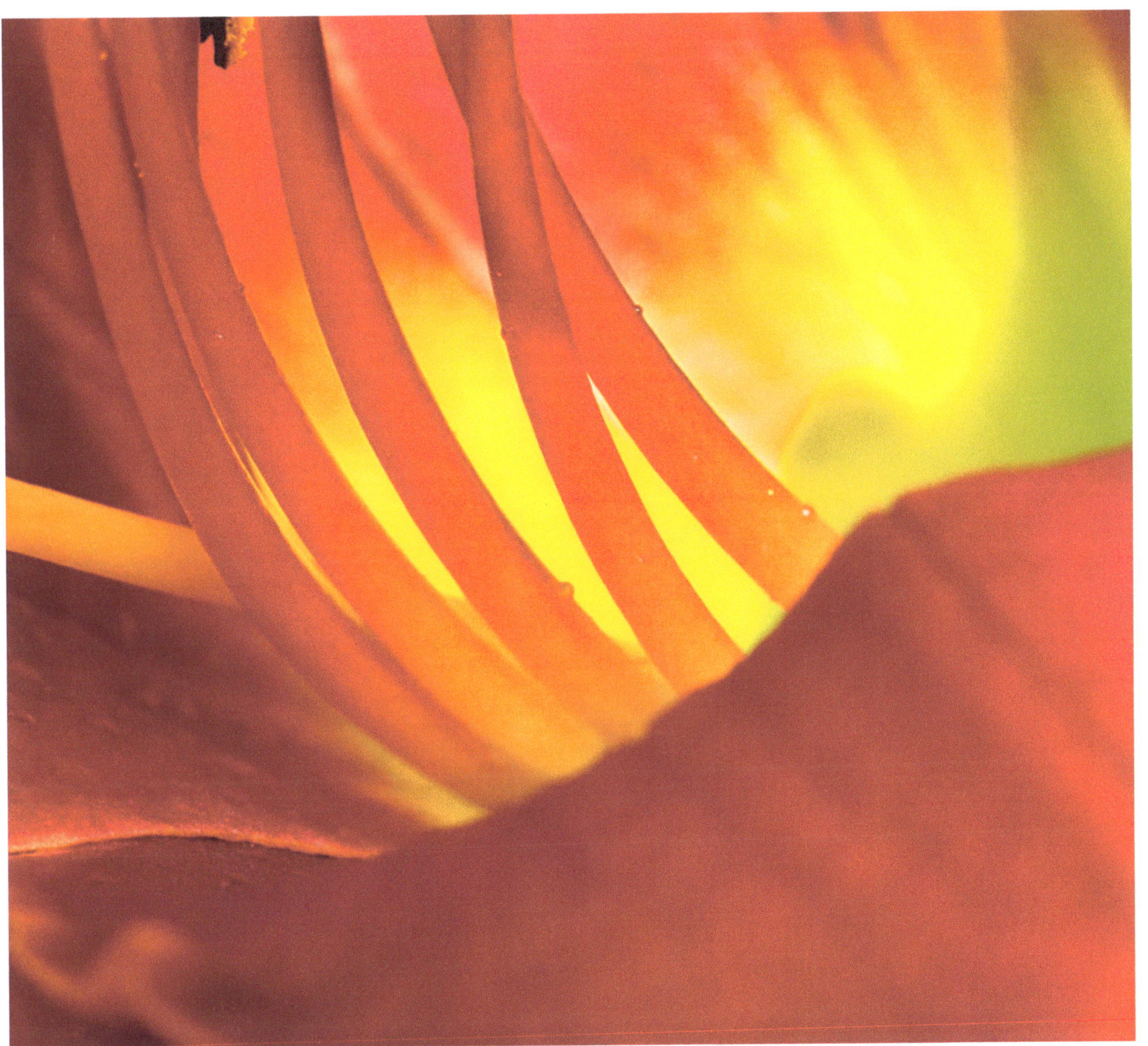

The center of an Iris flower.

Photographers love the blue hour after the sun sets, or before it rises.

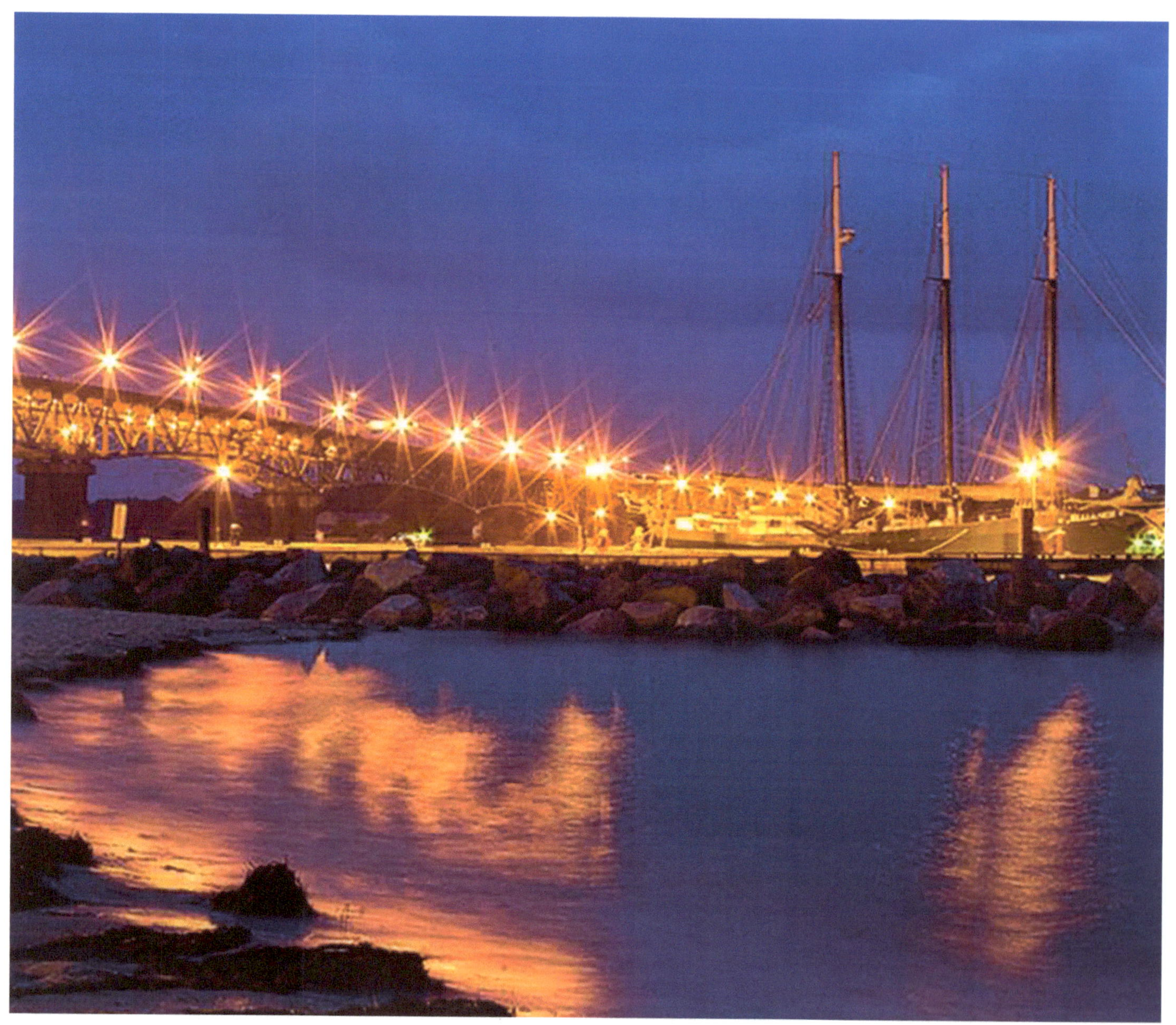

The blue hour at the Coleman Bridge in Yorktown, Virginia.

This photo captures the warm oranges and yellows in the sky during sunset.

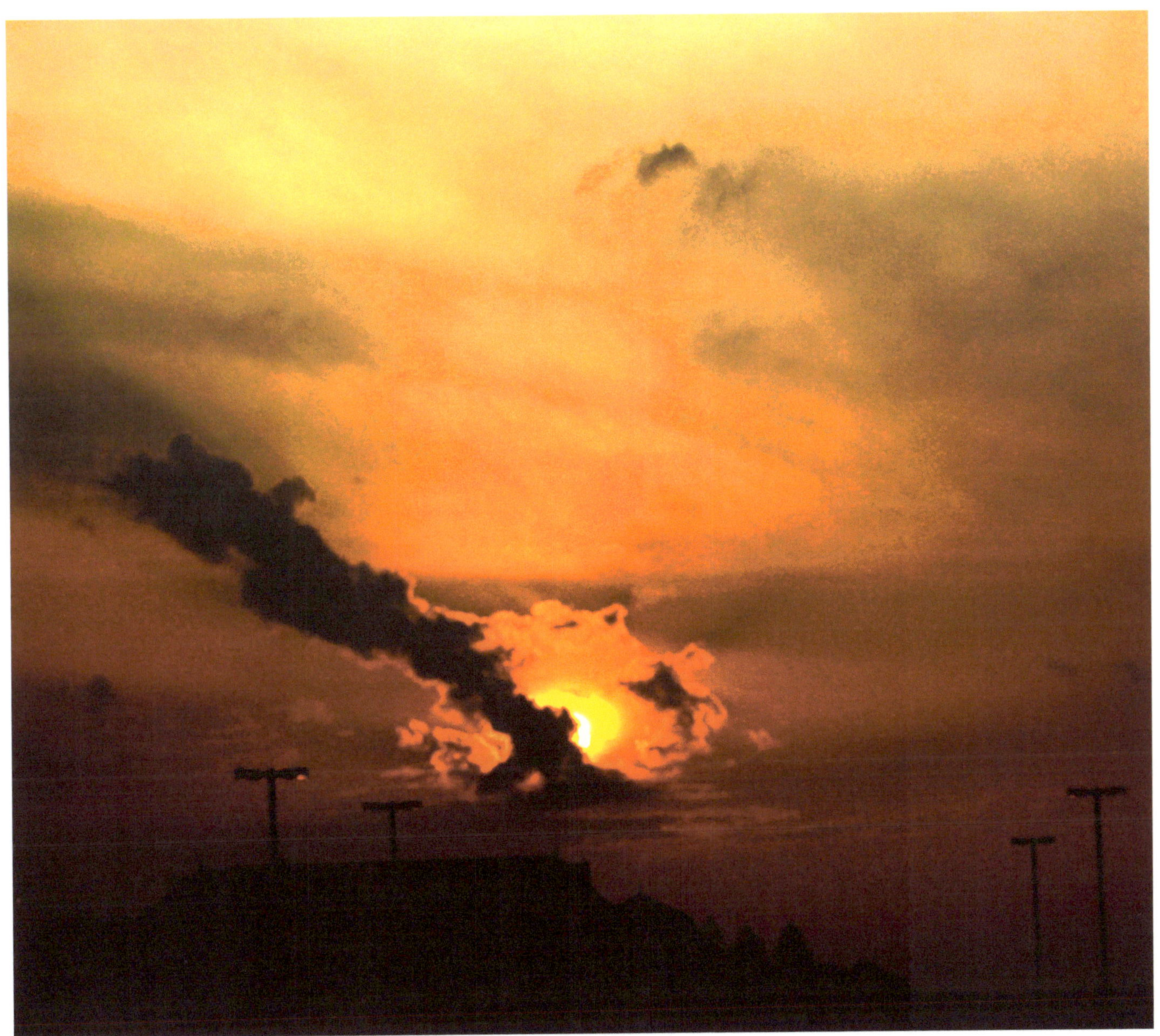

Sunset after a rainy day.

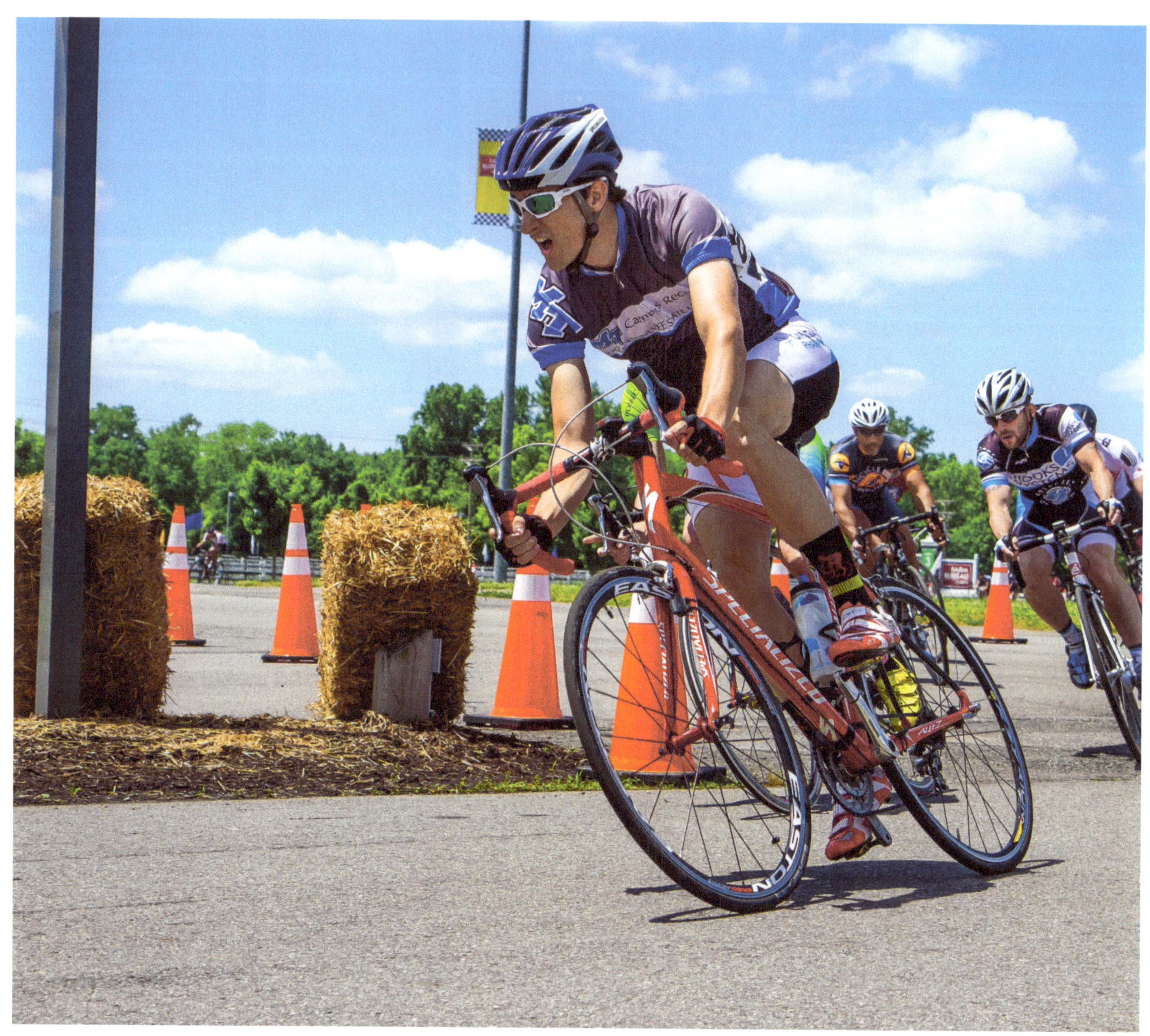

Ryan McGiboney racing in a criterium in Virginia.

And sometimes a peaceful silence.

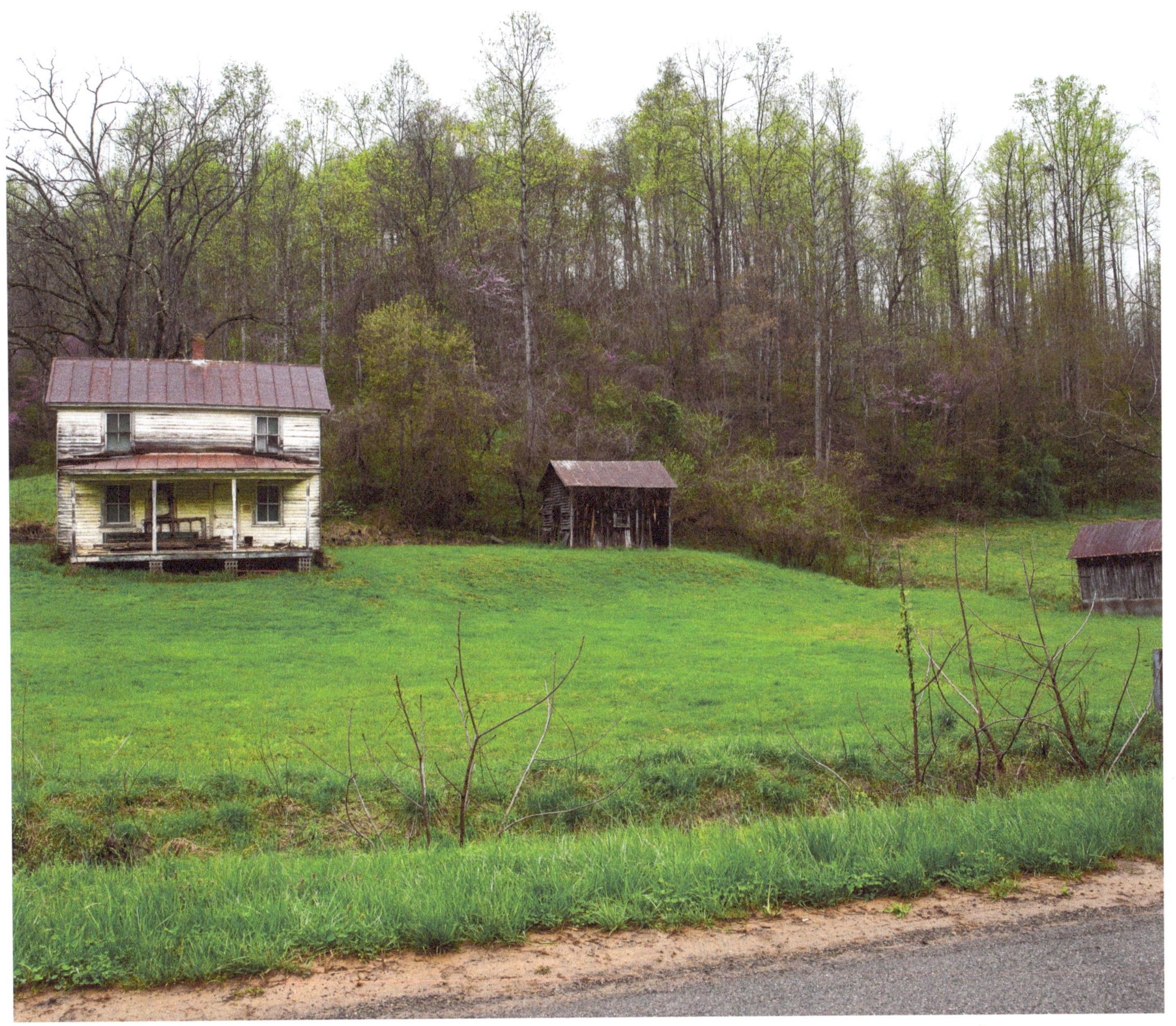

An abandoned property in Virginia.

Photos record history!

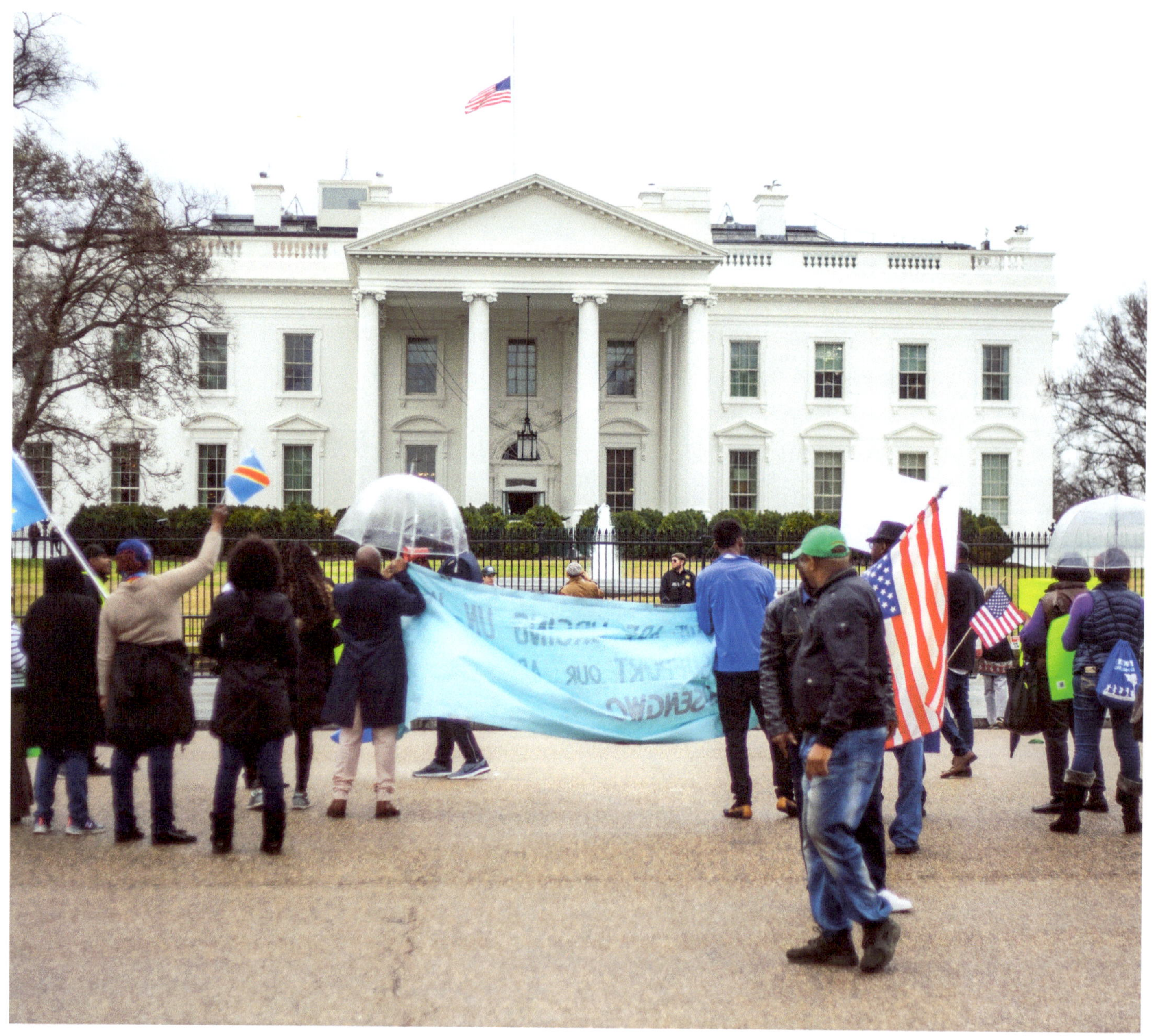

A march in Washington, D.C.

They show sadness.

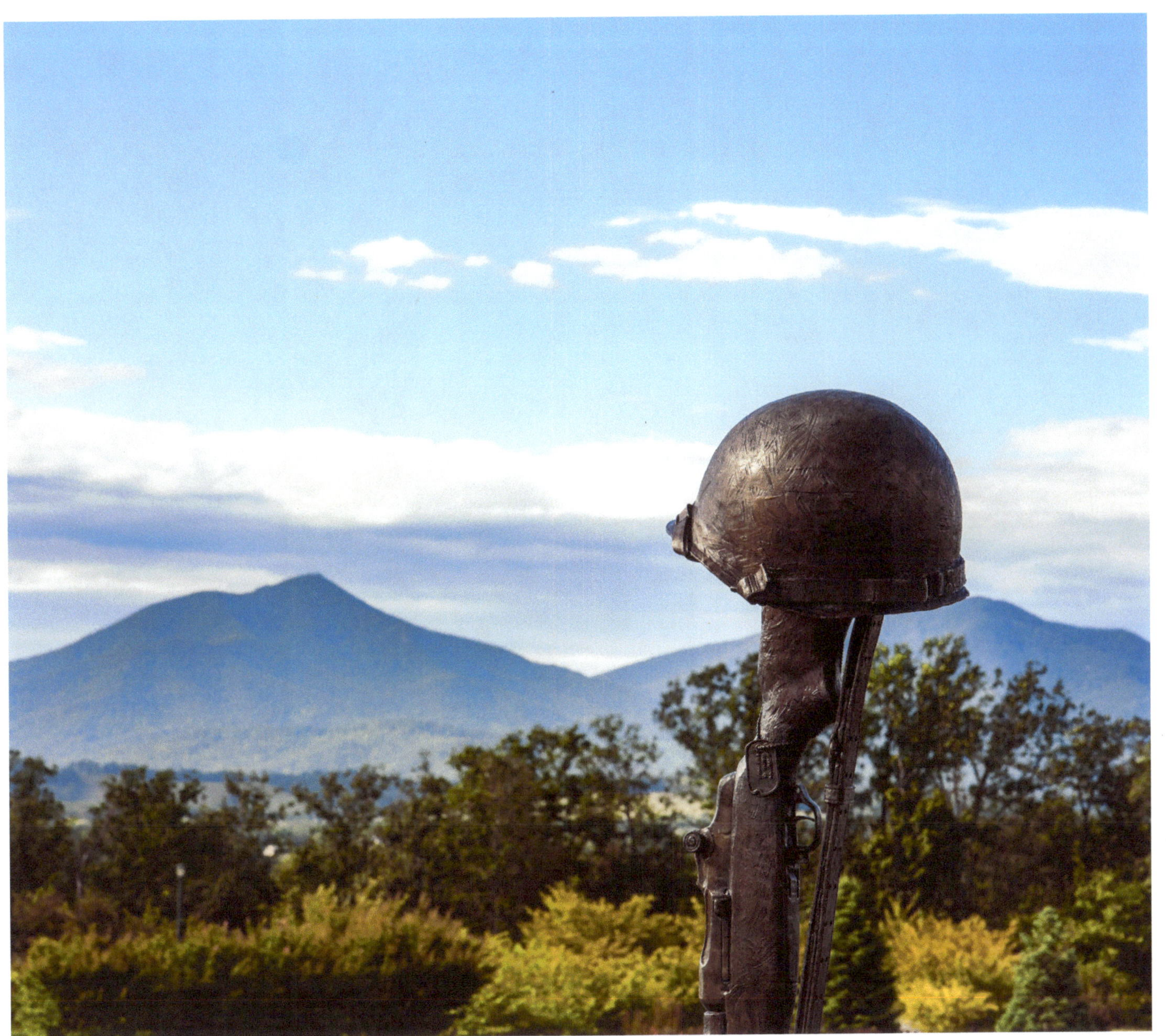

D-Day Memorial in Bedford, Virginia

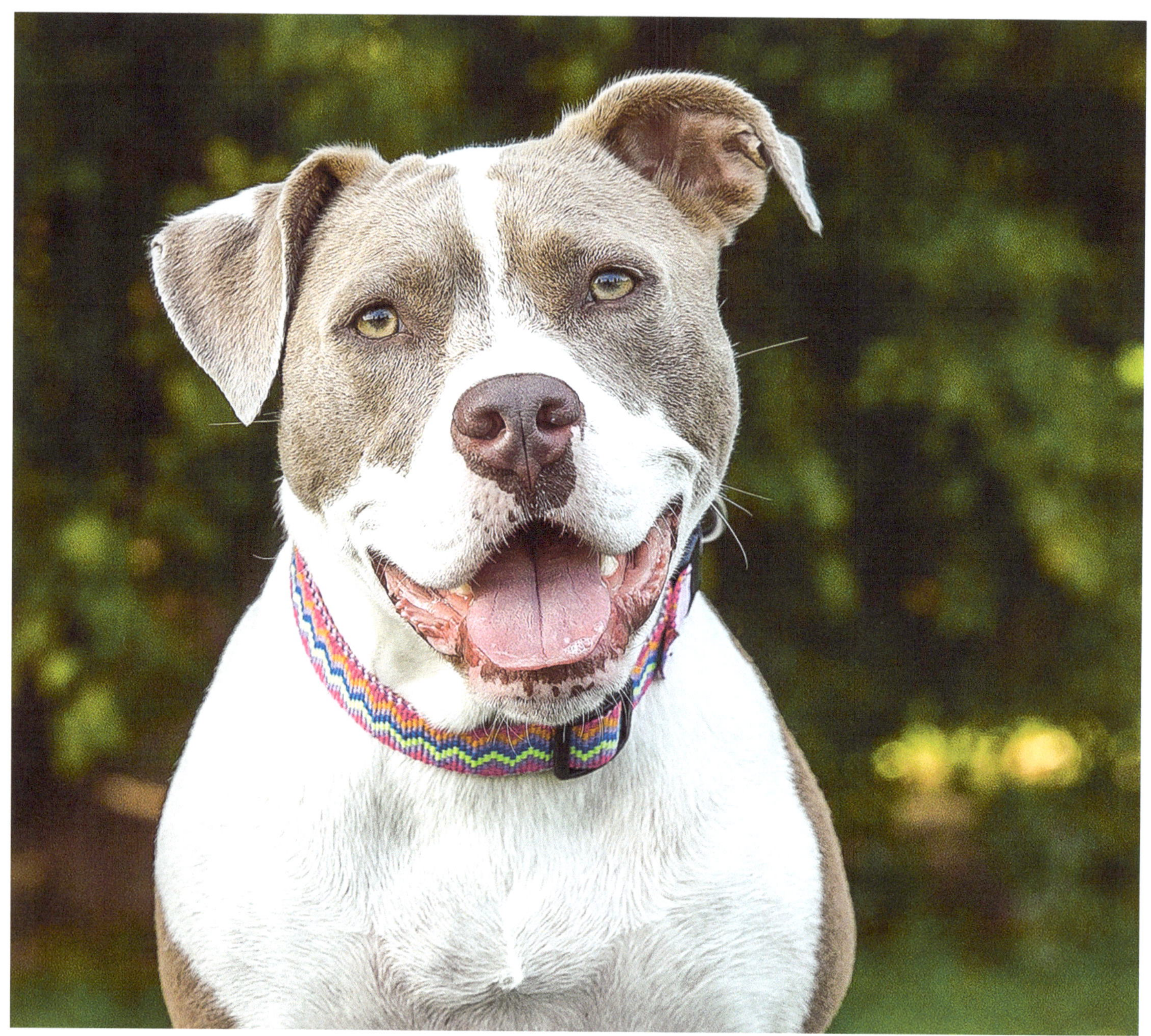

Jazzy!

They record celebrations.

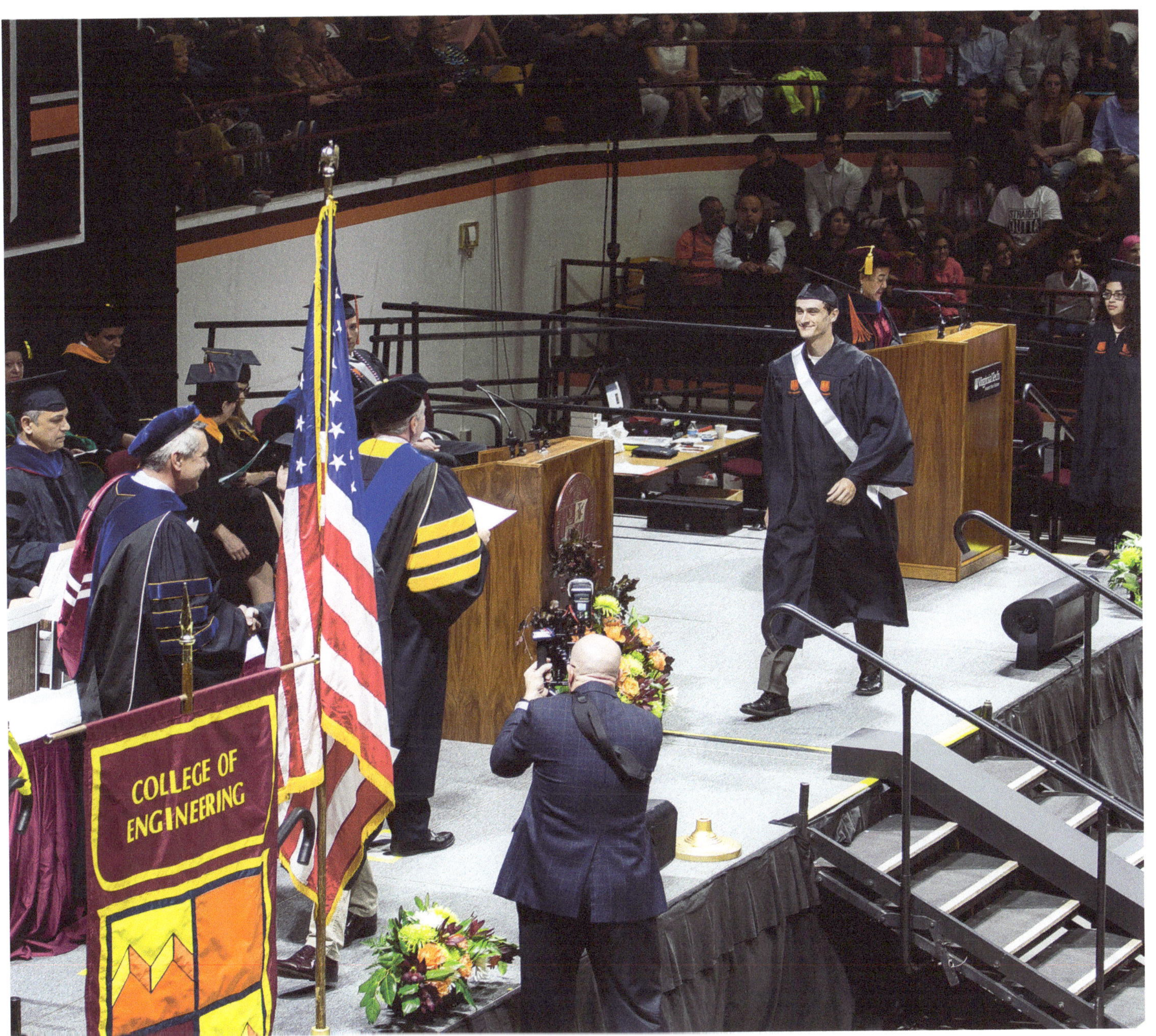

Ryan's college graduation.

Photos show love.

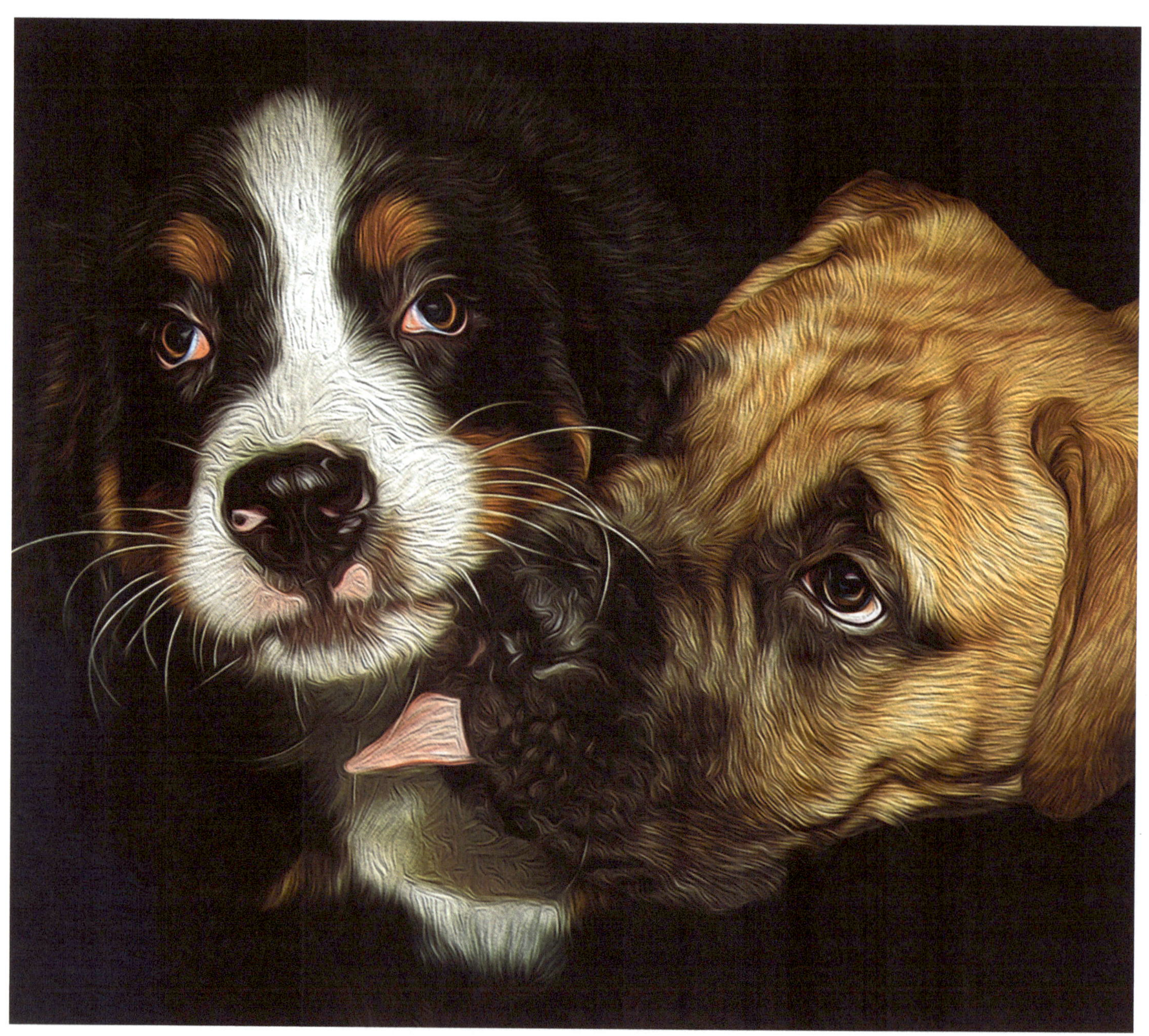

Two puppies becoming friends.

They tell stories. What does this picture tell you?

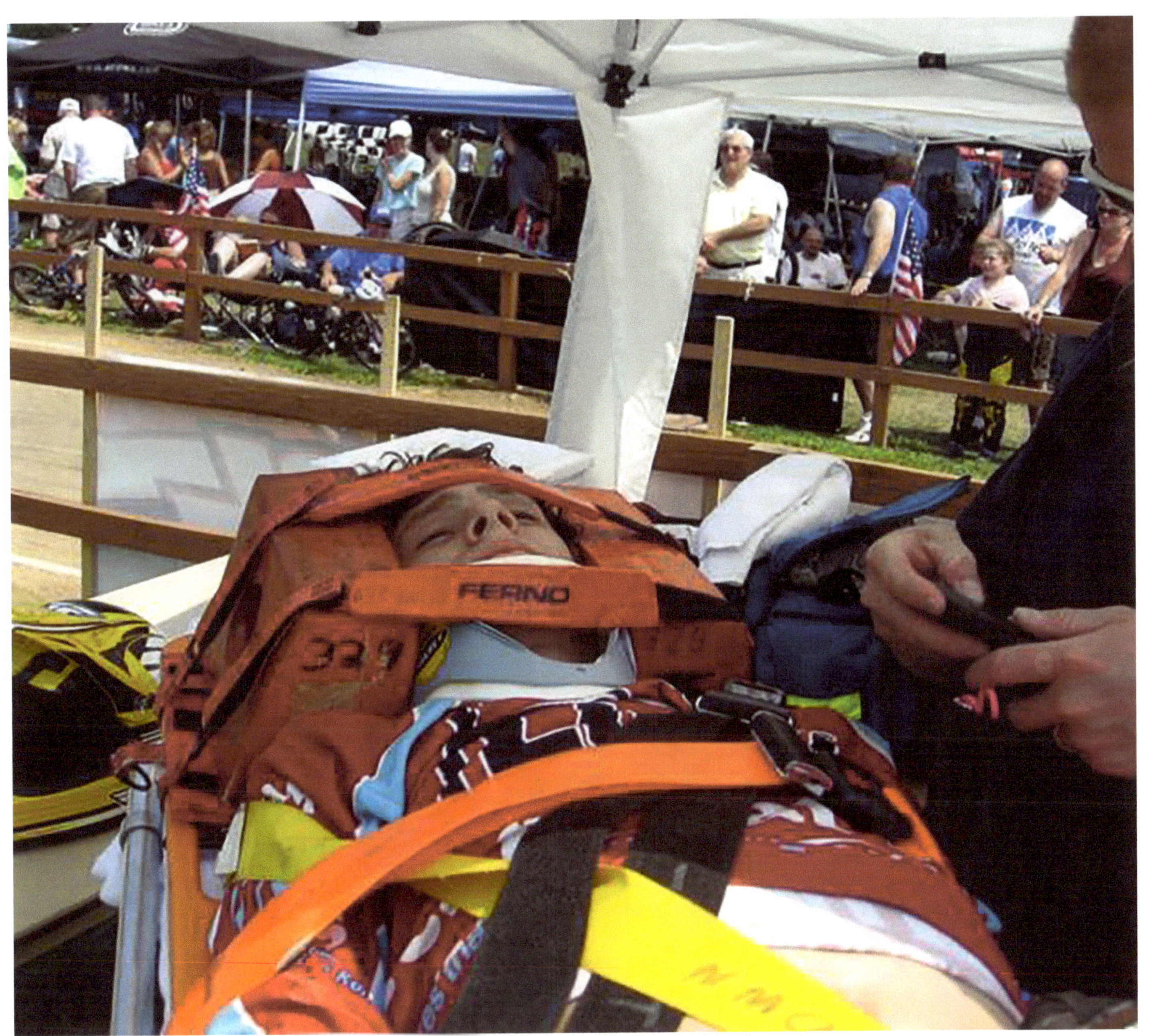

A crash during a BMX bike race.

Can you see a story in this picture?

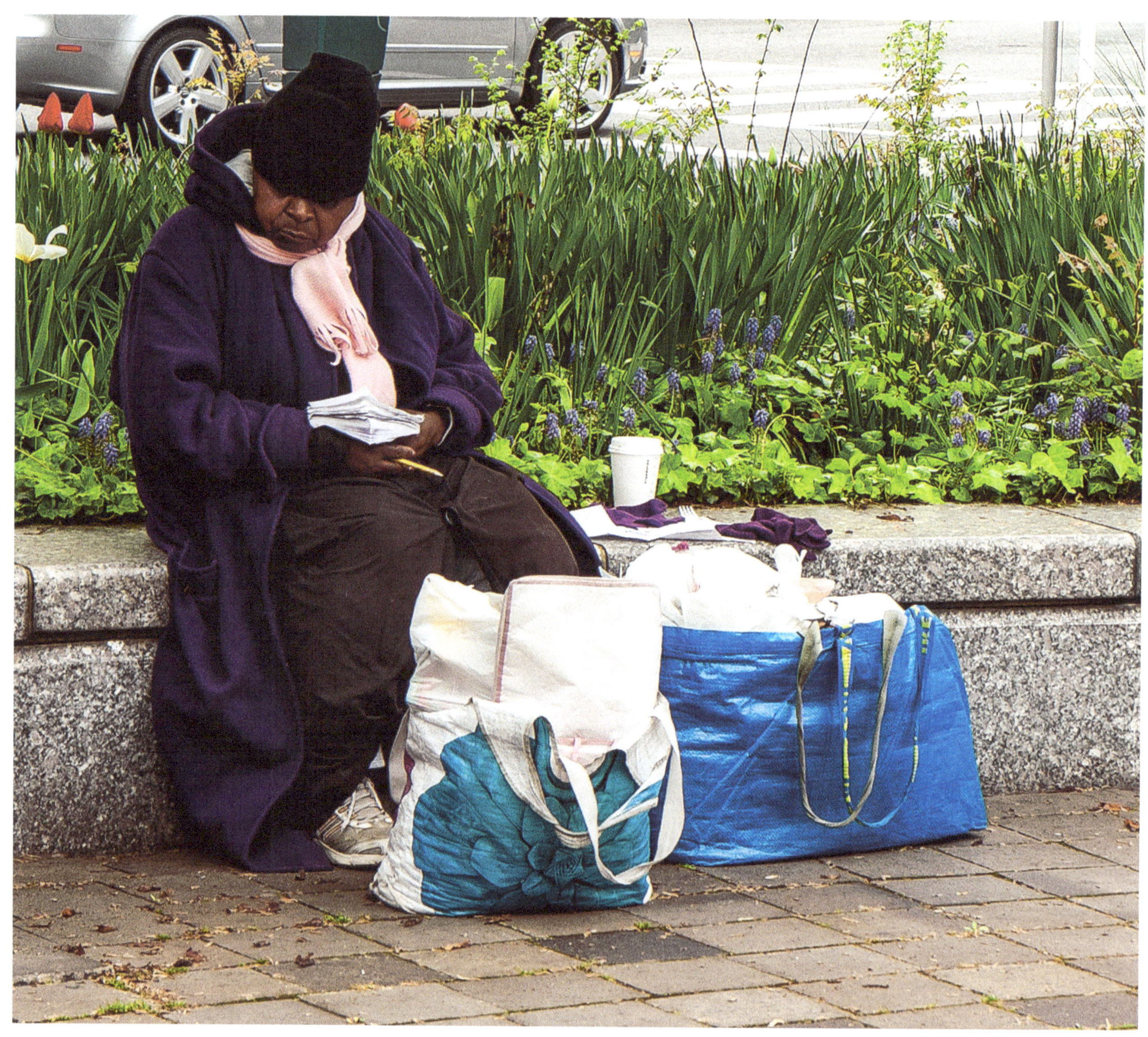

Waiting in Washington, D.C.

You can take pictures from different angles. This one is from low to the ground.

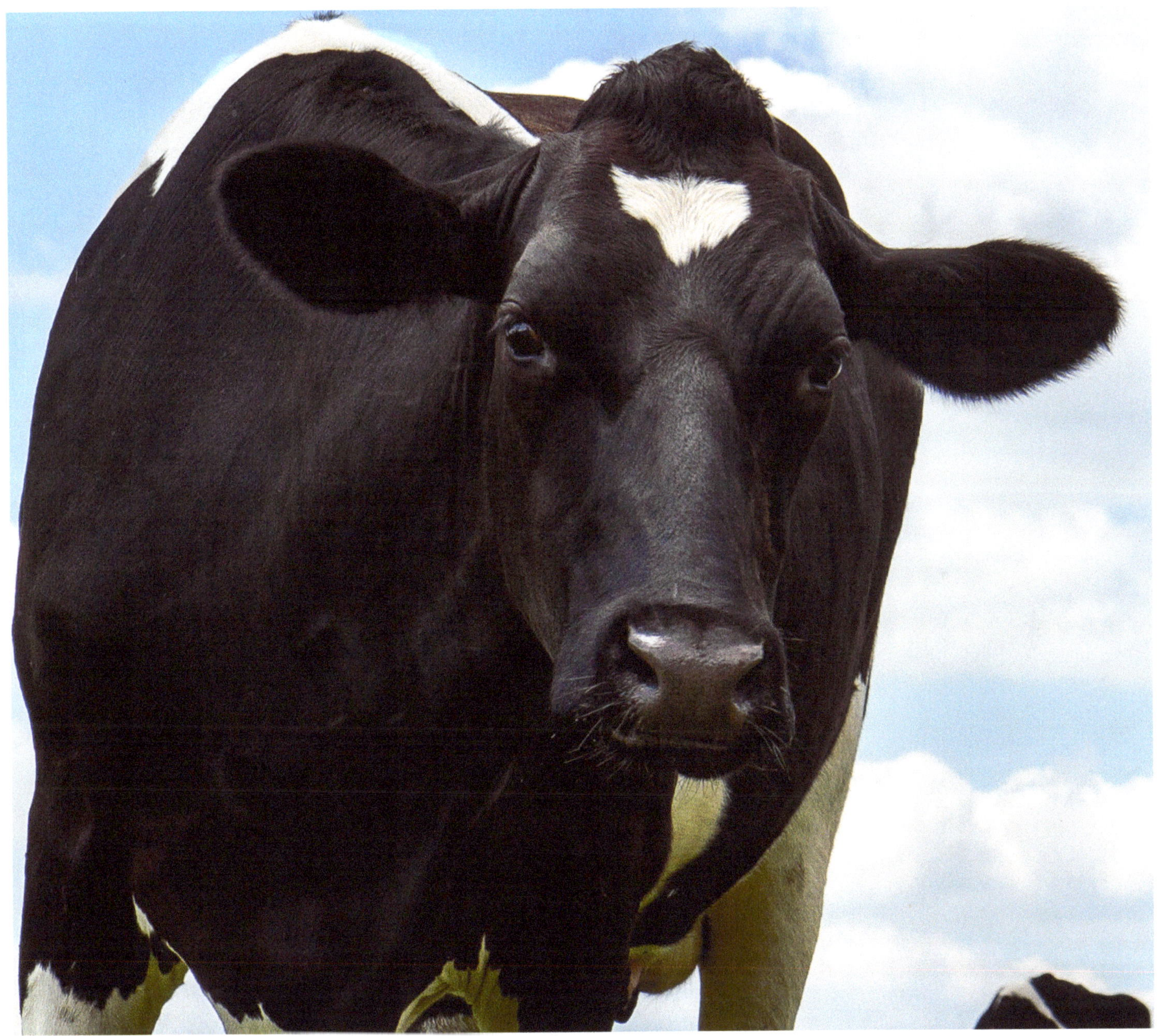

Cows are curious and come right up to the fence when I take their pictures.

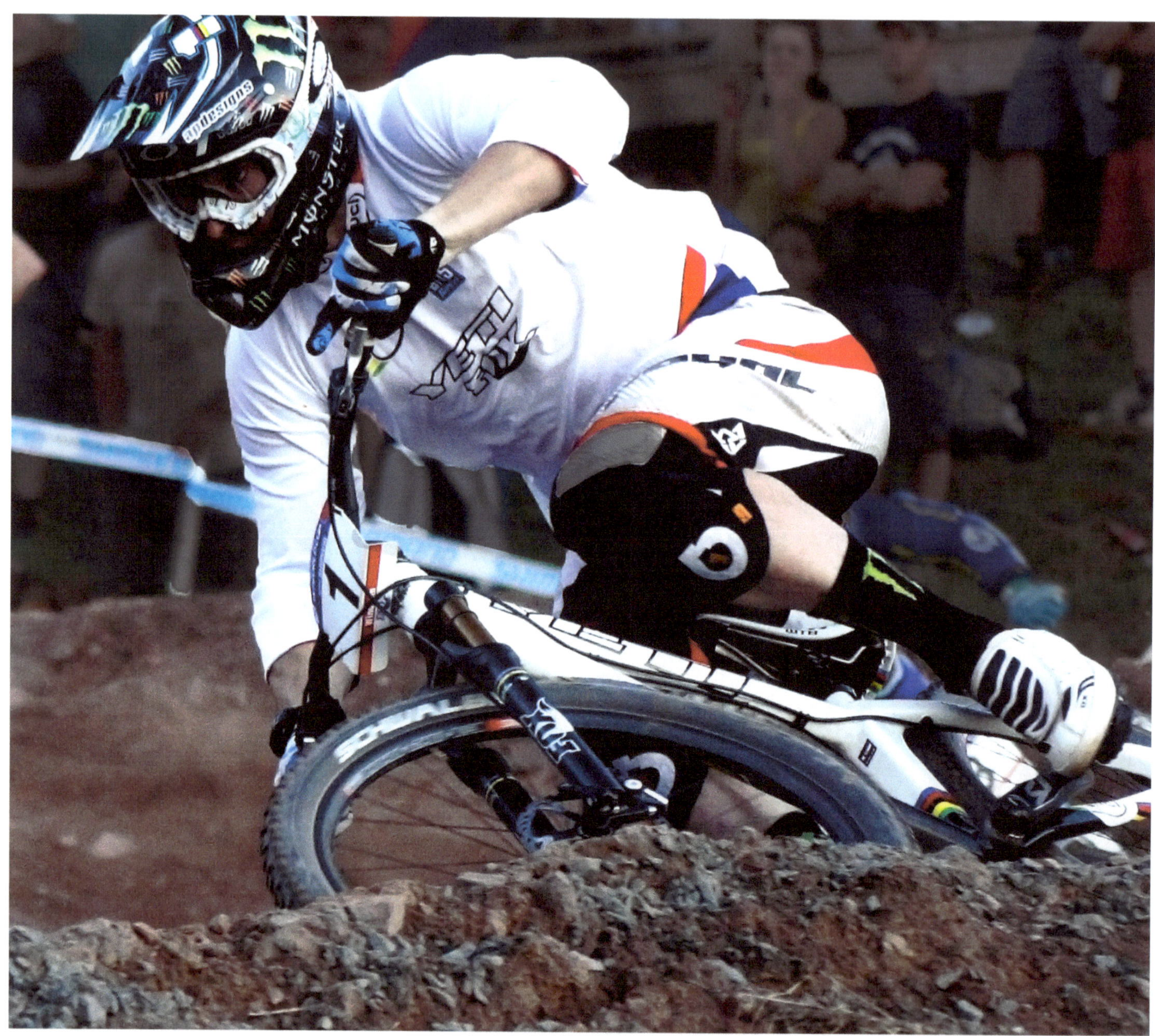

A slalom race at Windham Mountain's Bike Park in New York, 2010.

Pictures taken from above, and zoomed out, add more detail about the story.

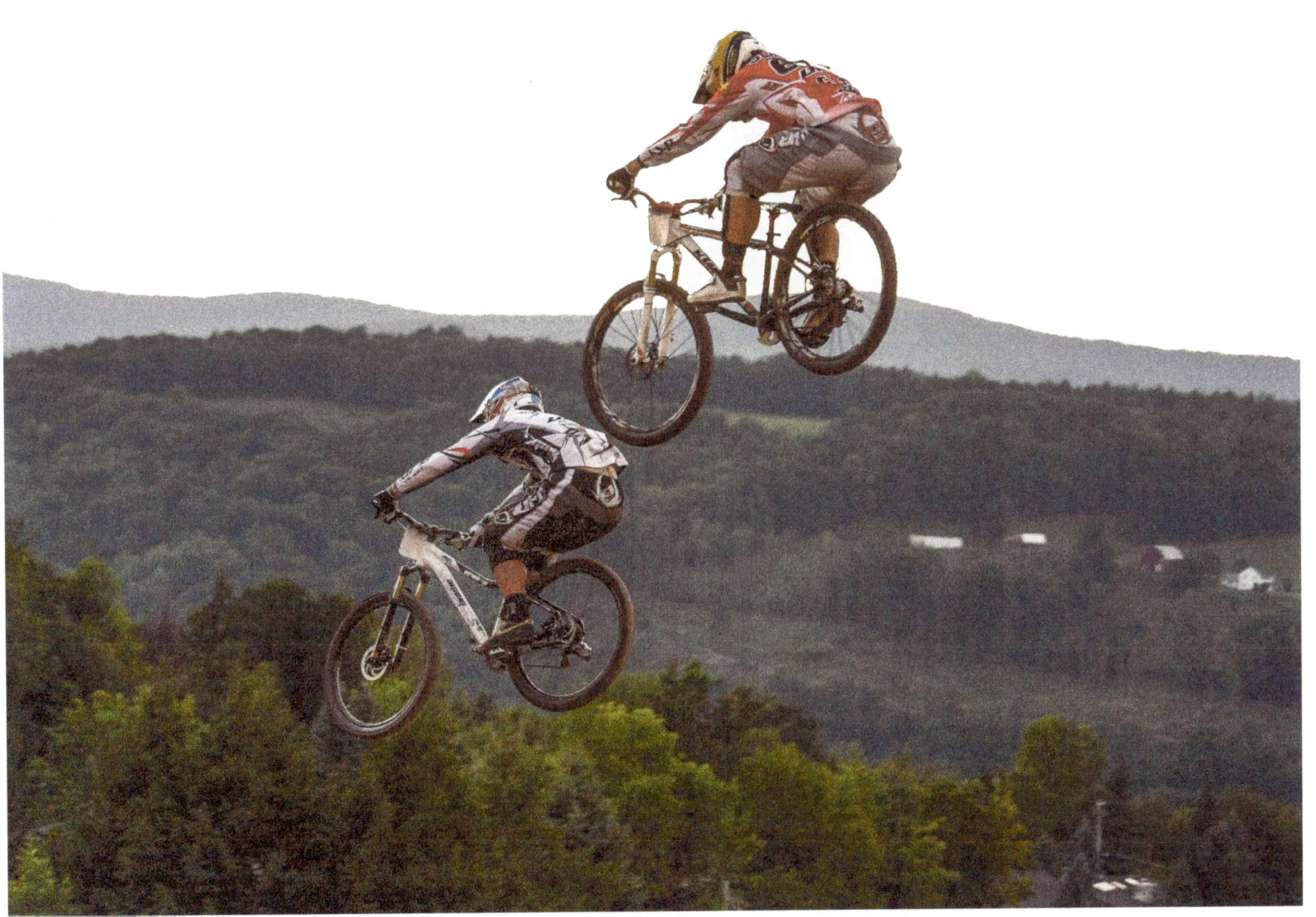

World Cup Downhill Race, 2010

Use objects to frame things. See how the trees make a circle around the castle.

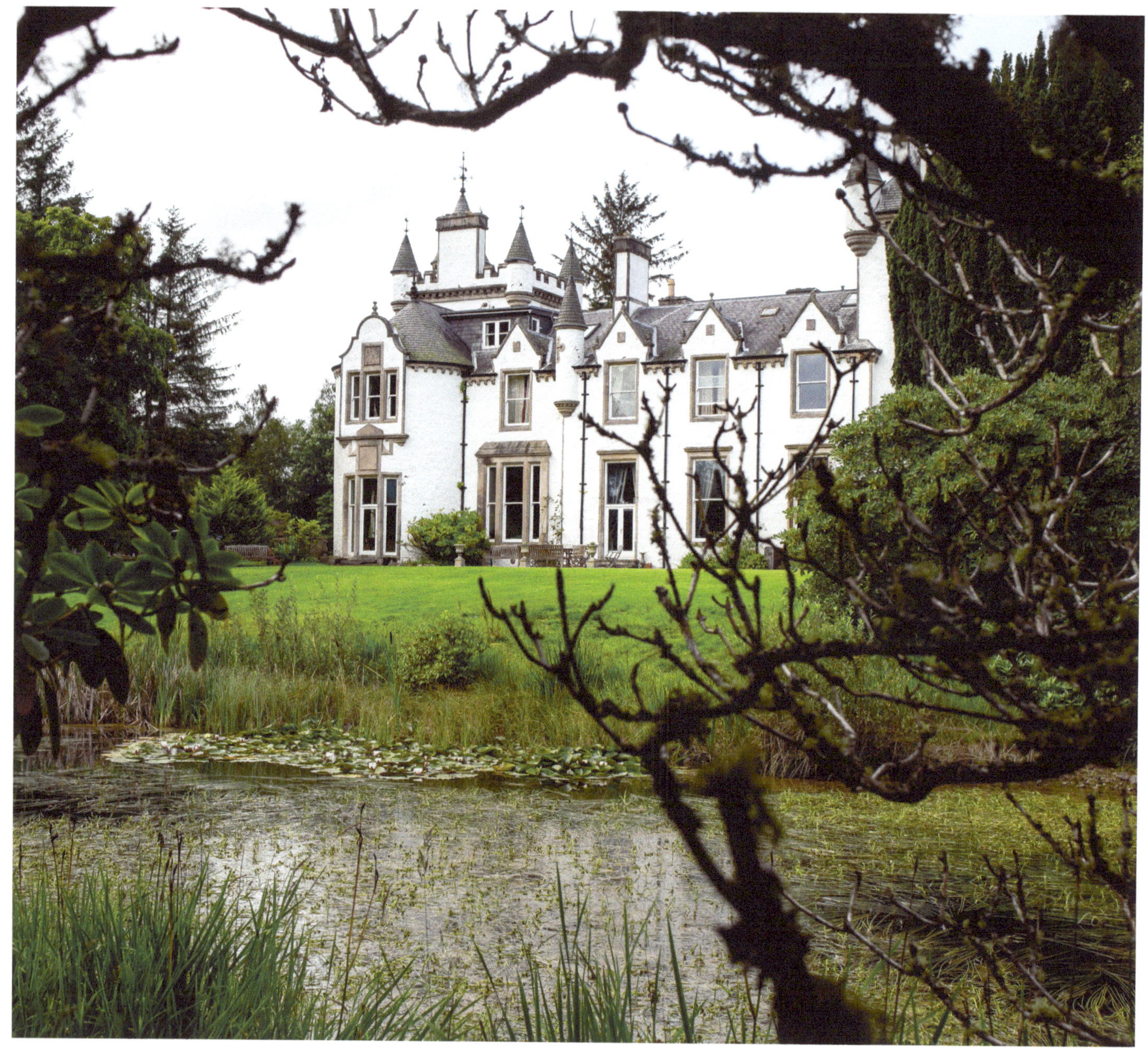

Dalnaglar Castle, Scotland, 2023

Include more background to give more of the story.

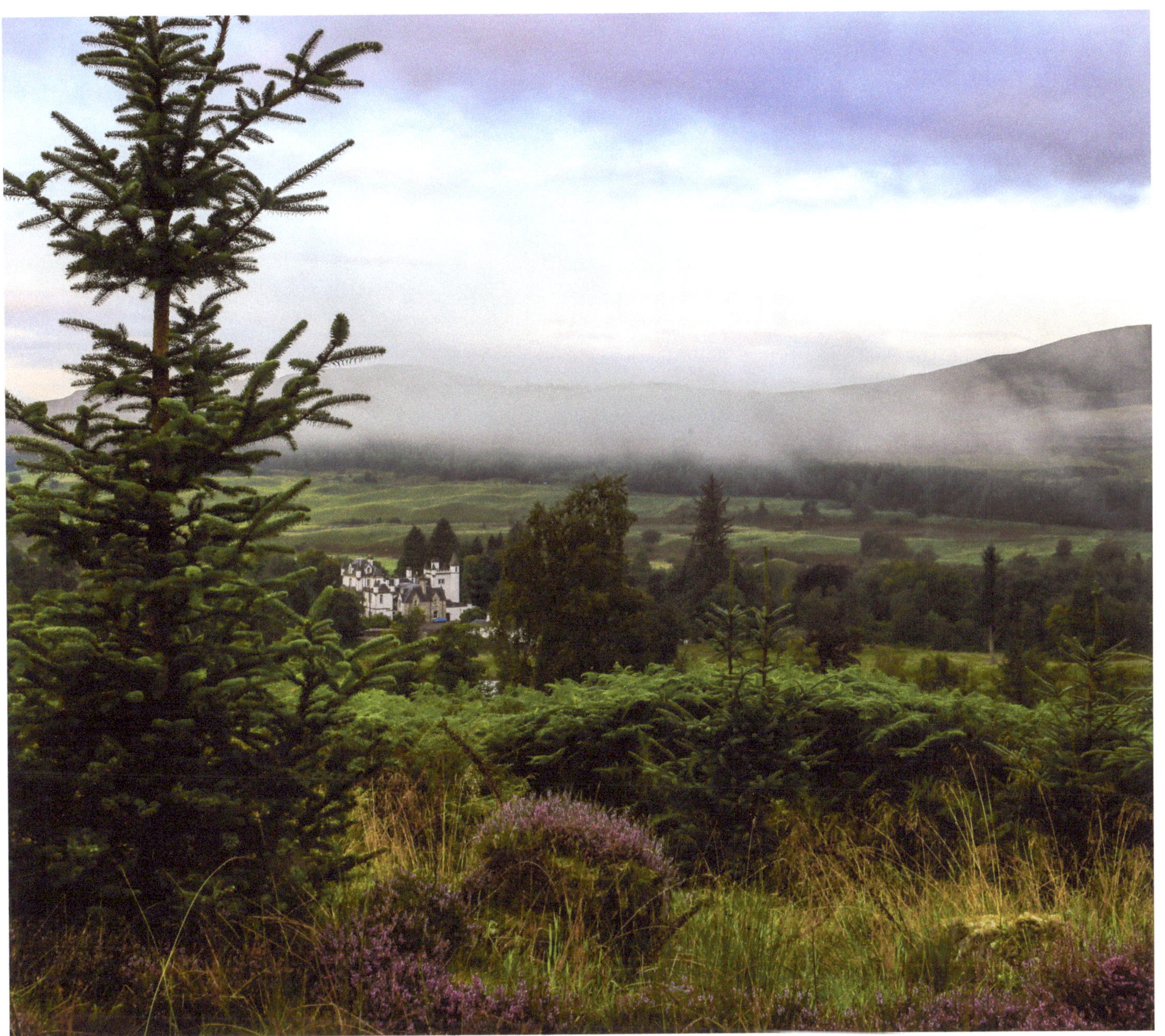

The meadows and hills around the castle.

Images can be taken so that every detail is visible and sharp.

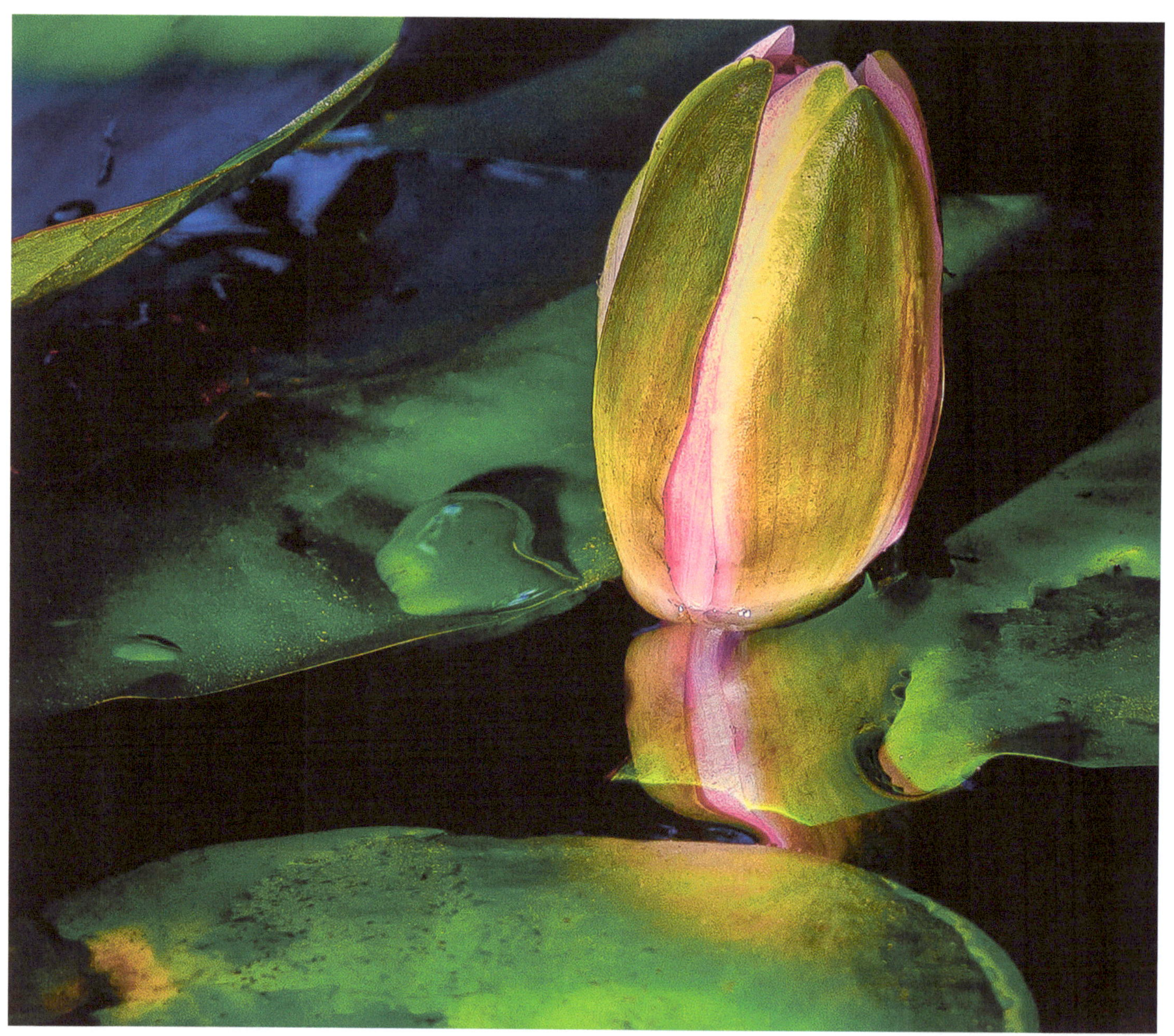

A water lily and lily pads. Can you imagine a frog in this picture?

But sometimes it's cool to blur the motion.

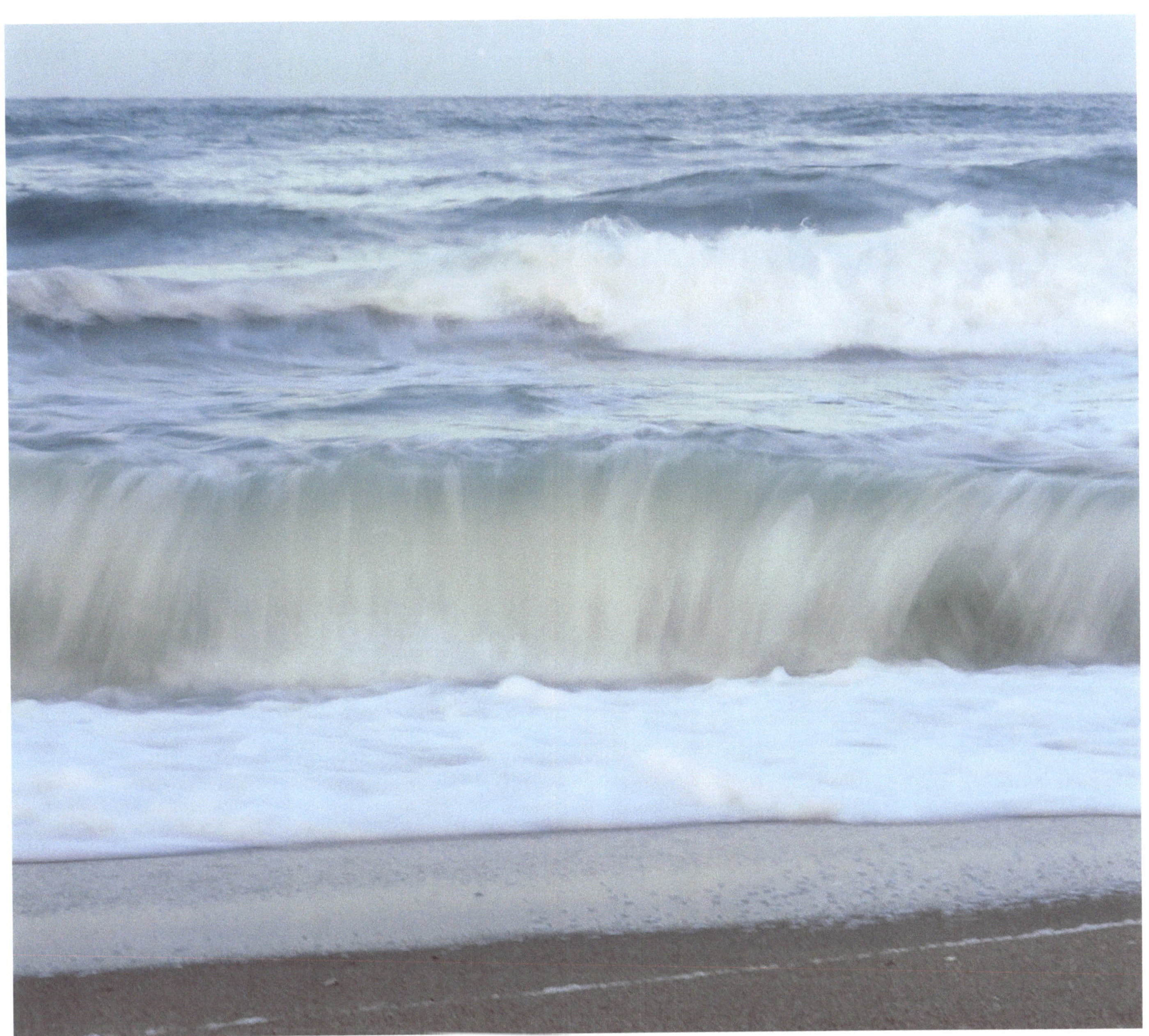

Rolling waves in Kill Devil Hills, North Carolina.

Light, from different angles, creates shadows and sometimes glowing edges.

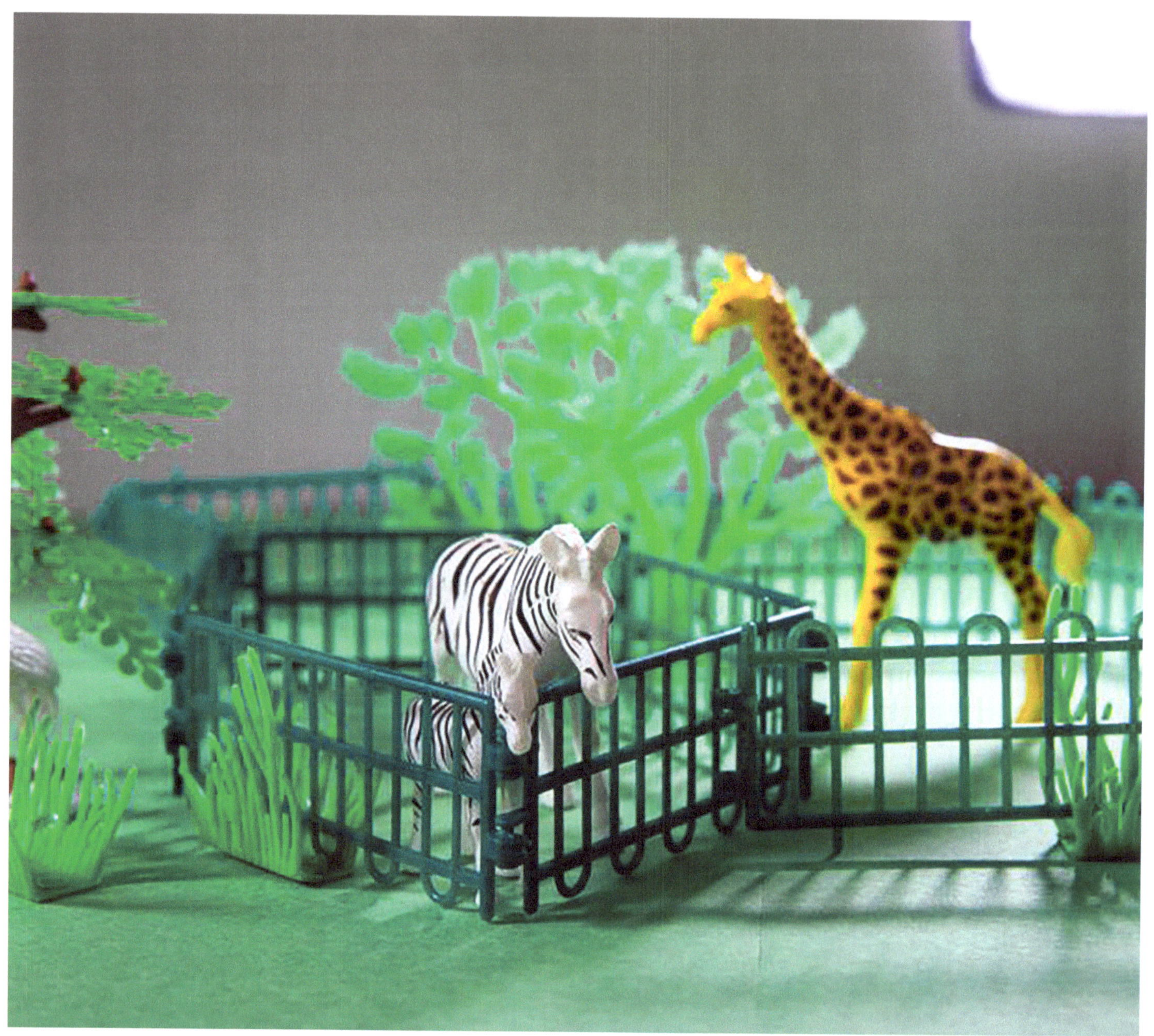

Use props to practice using light.

Light in the front of a subject will eliminate shadows on the subject.

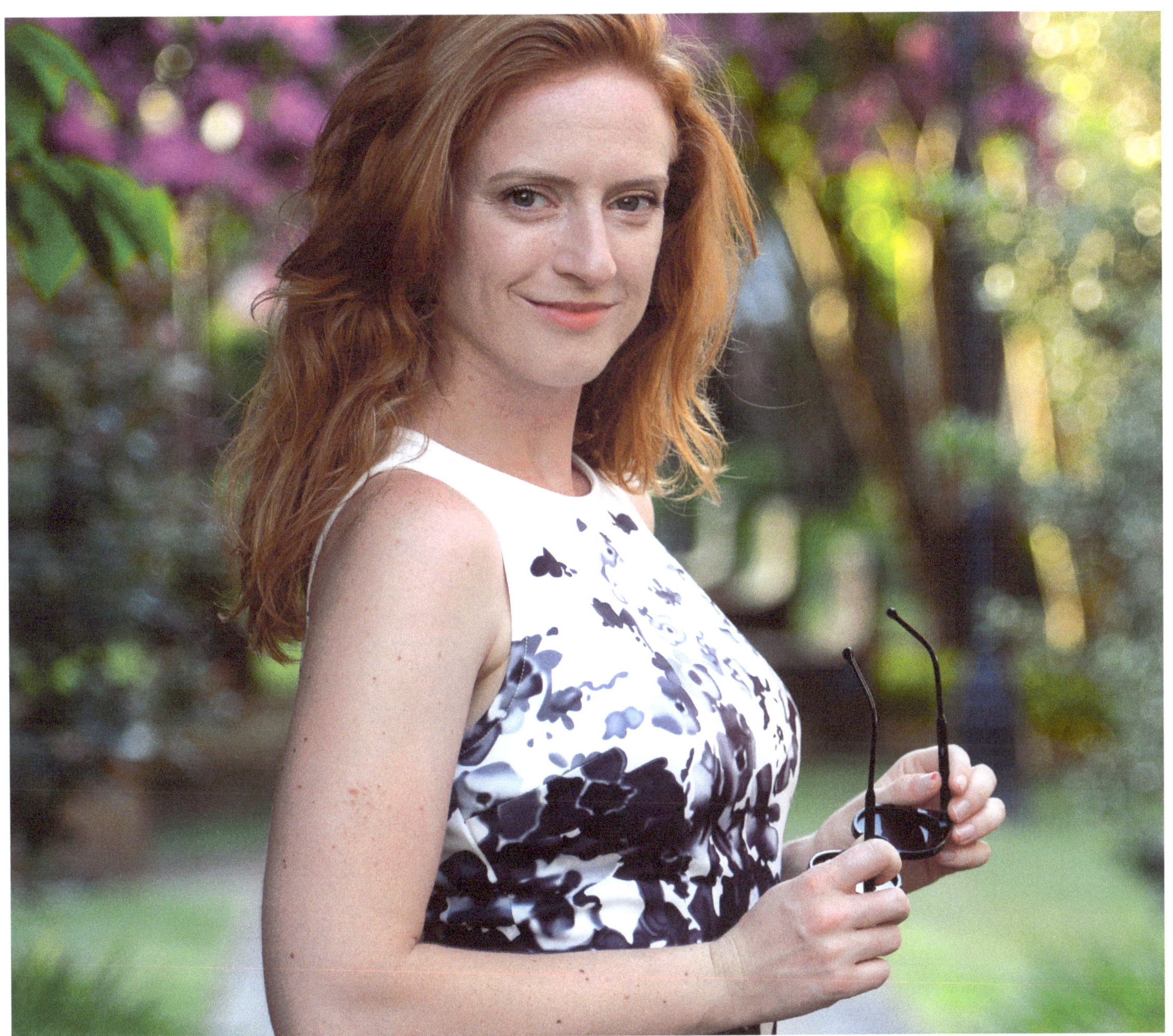

Rachel posing for a portrait.

Light that is low, like the rising or setting sun, makes tall shadows.

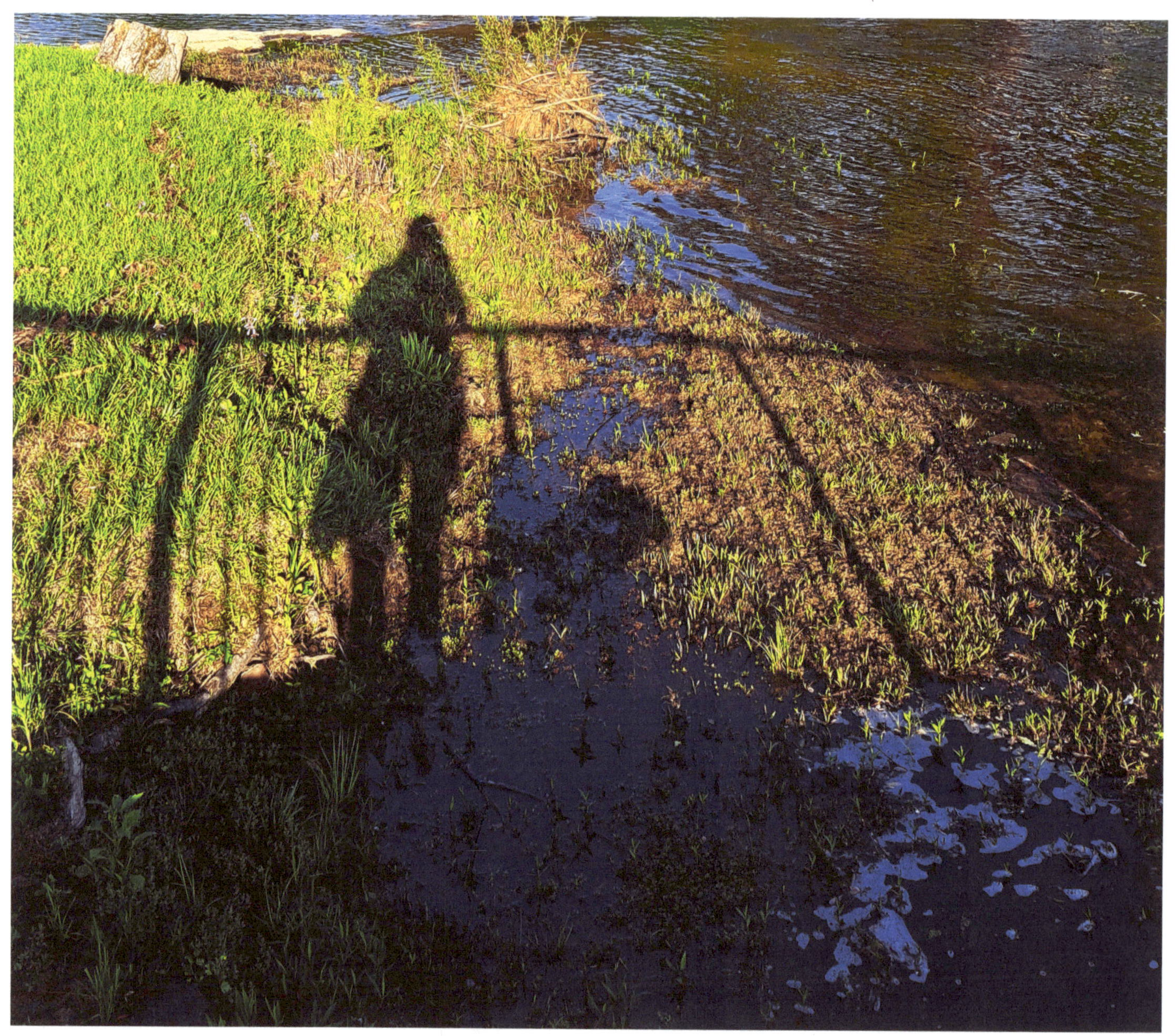

Sonja and Jazzy on the bridge at Noccalula Falls Park in Gadsden, Alabama.

Light that comes from high above makes small shadows.

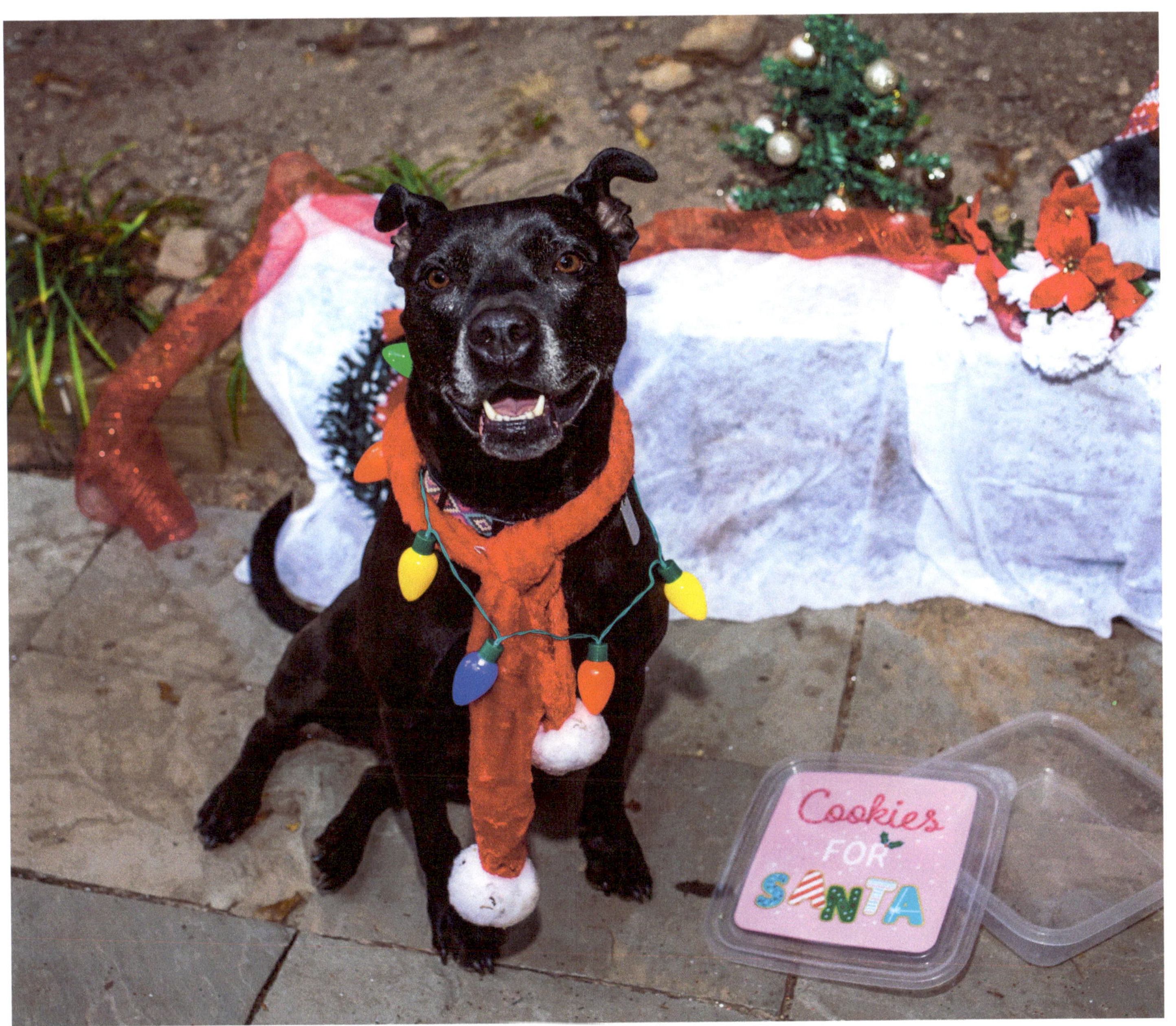

My dog Evie posing for her Christmas card.

Light from behind a subject, called a back light, creates a silhouette.

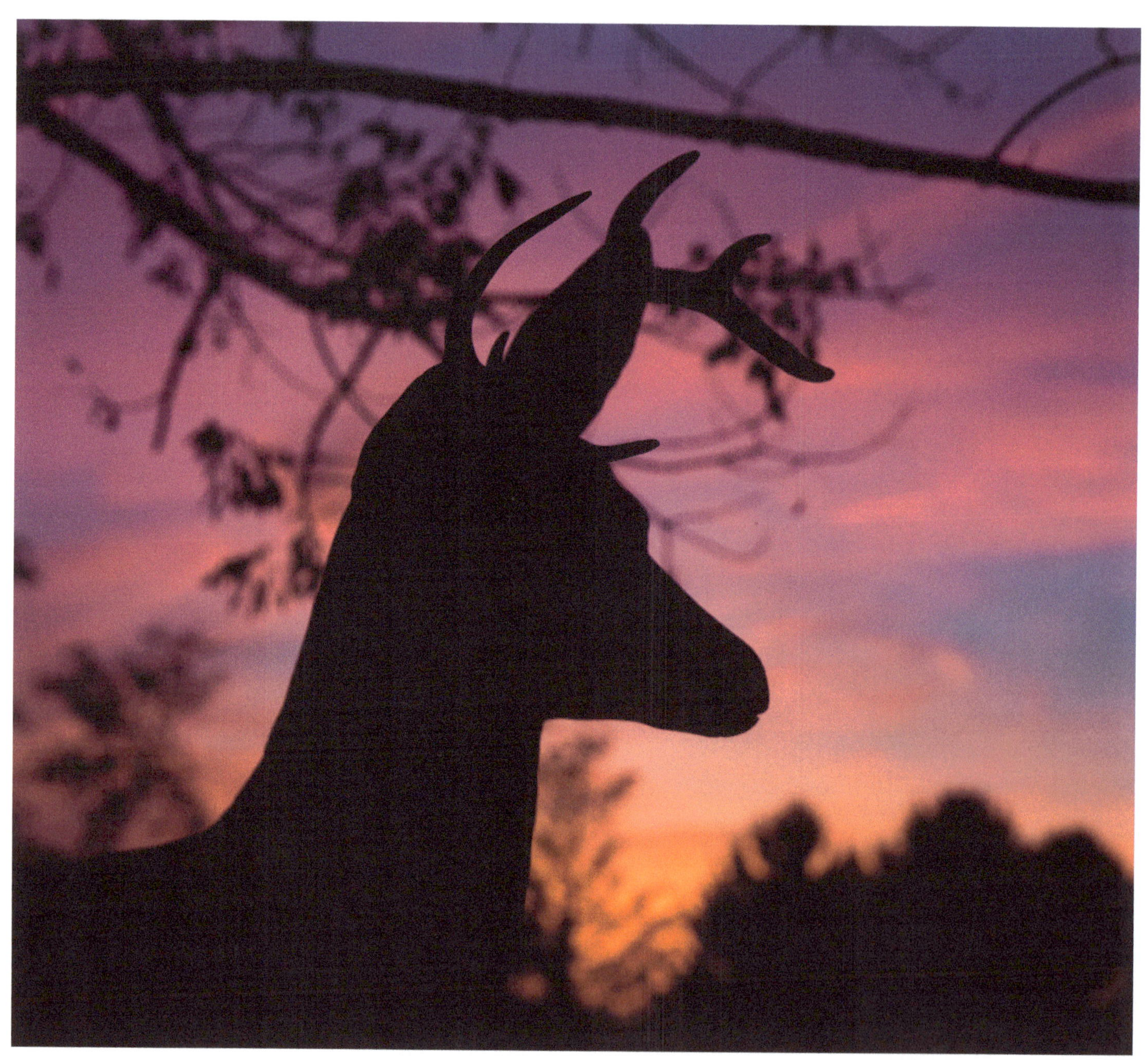

A statue at the entrance to a home in Lancaster, Pennsylvania.

Daylight allows the photographer to see everything.

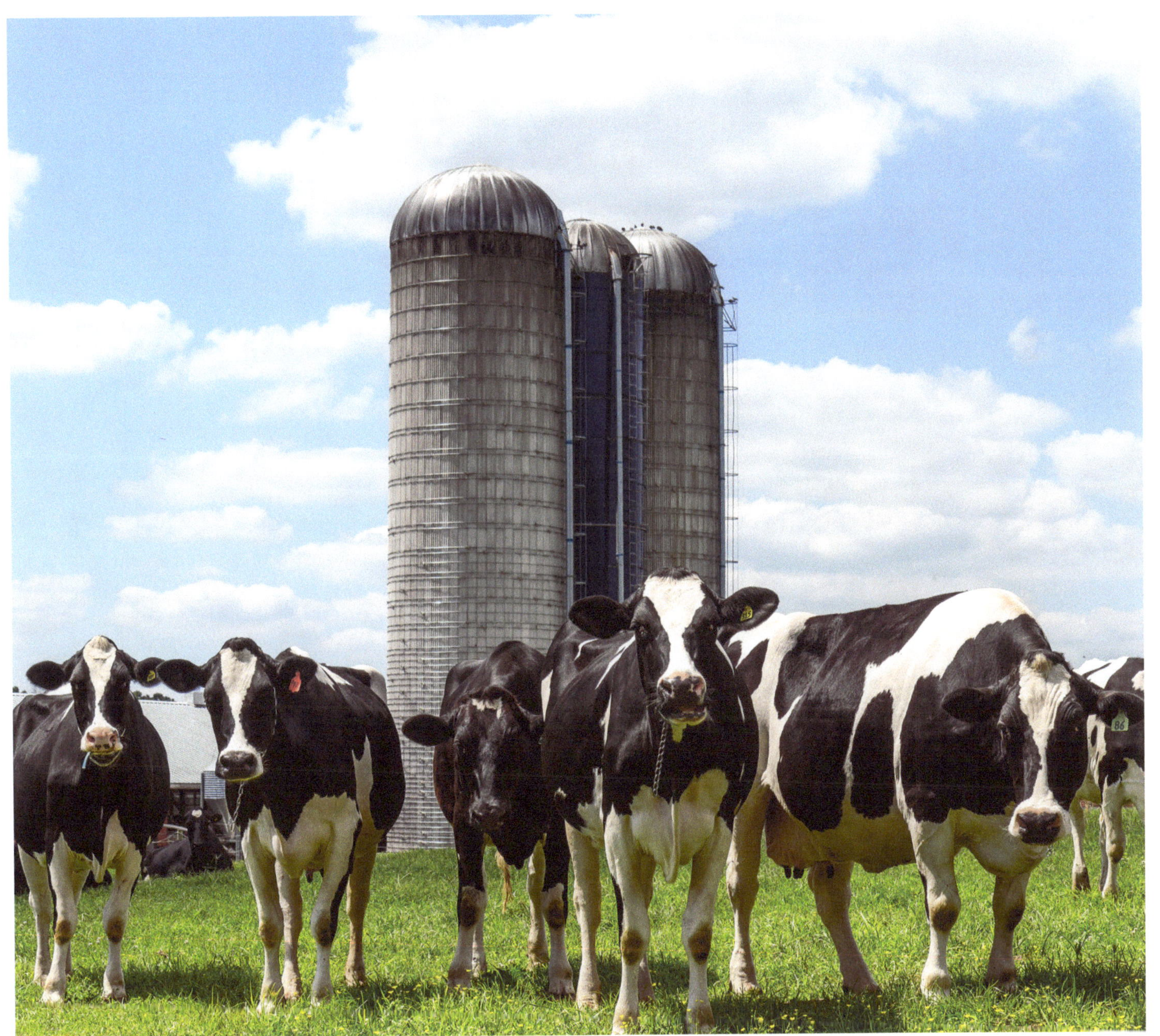

Curious cows congregating to stare at Sonja.

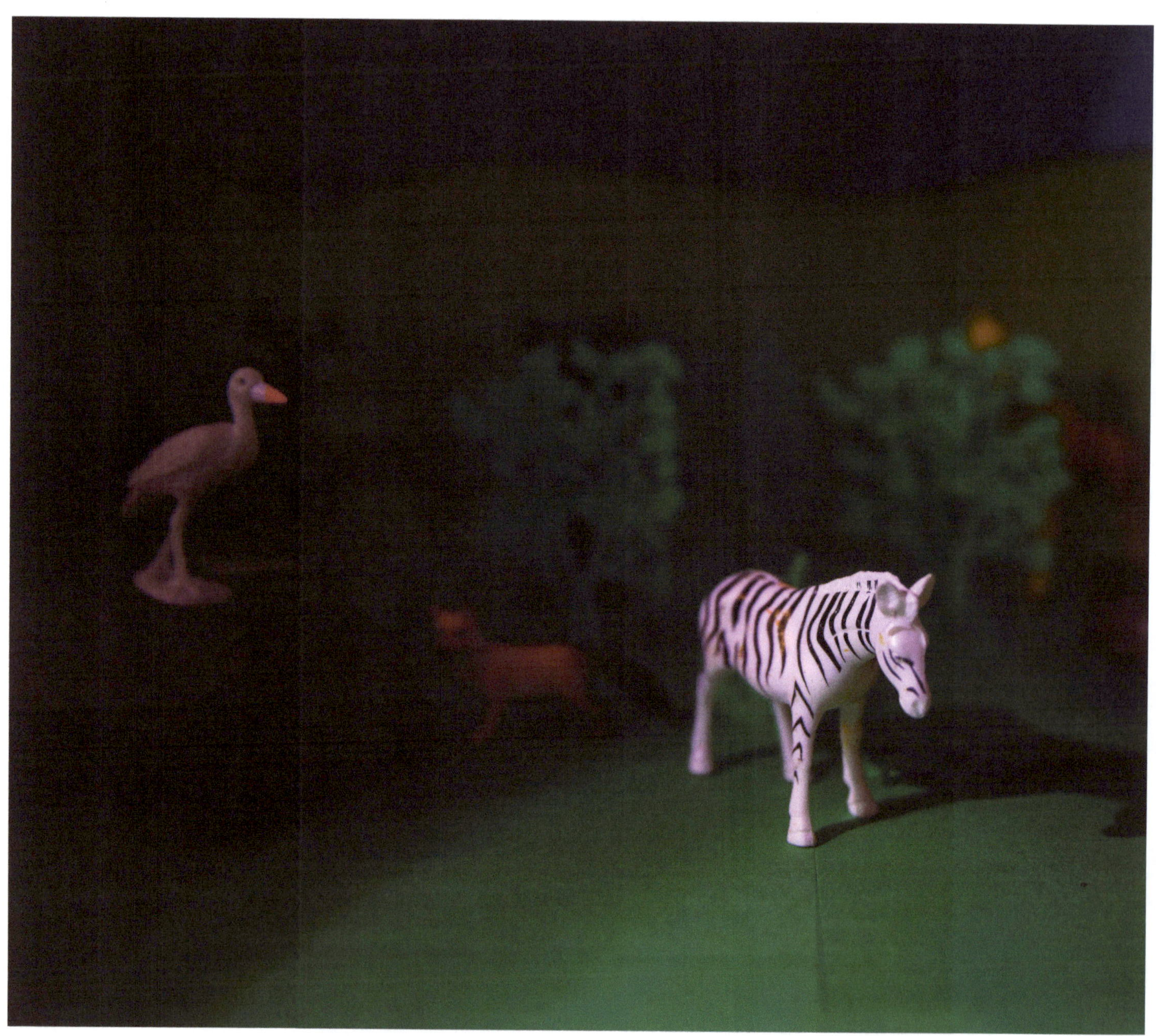

More photography practice using a flashlight and toys.

Finding patterns and textures can be fun.

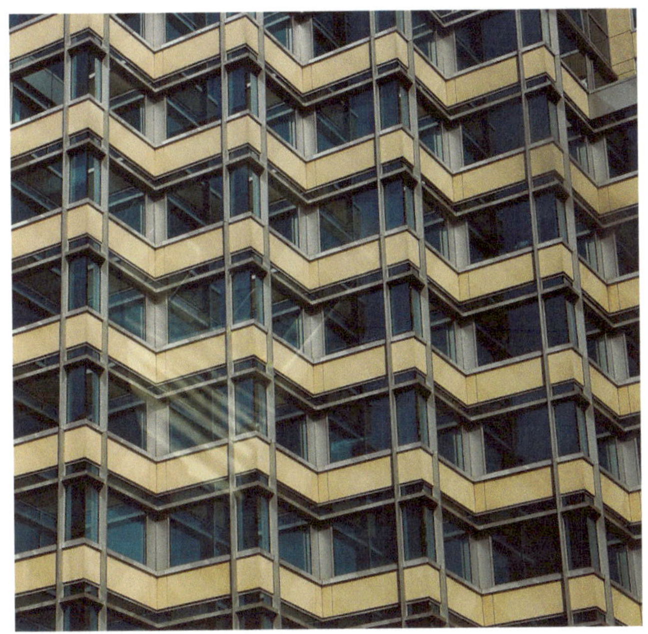

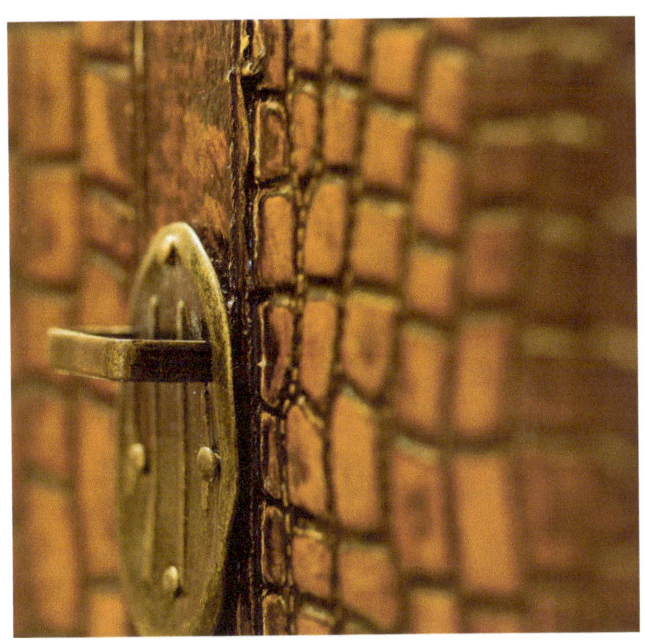

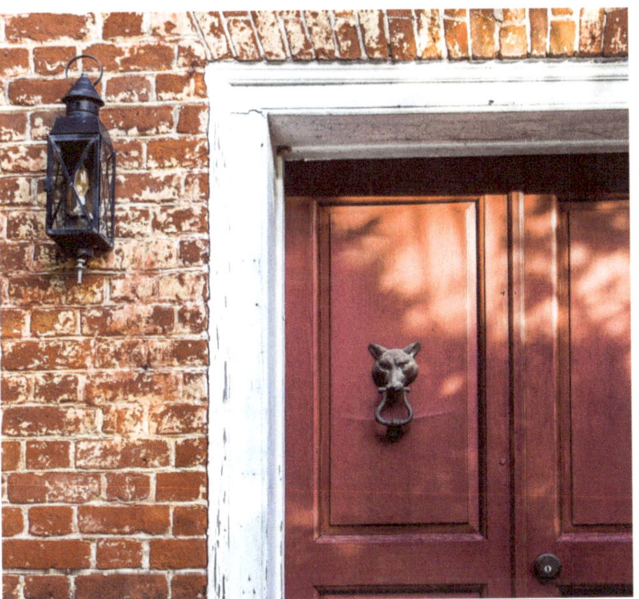

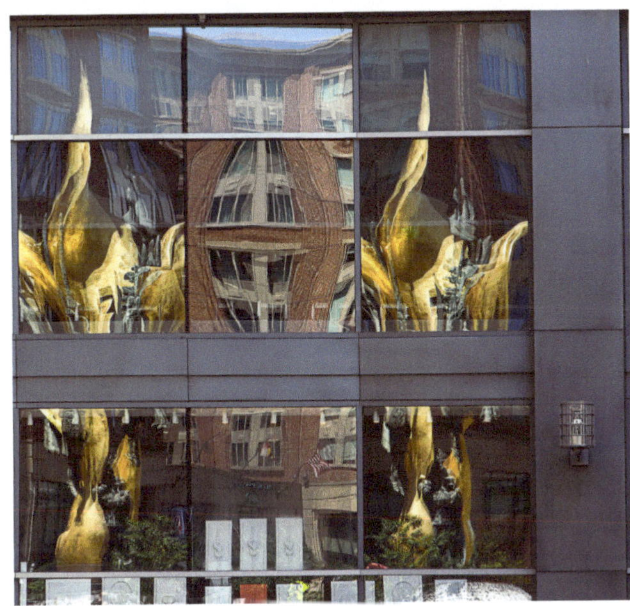

Buildings and purses provide great textures and patterns.

Turn the camera to get a portrait (up and down) orientation.

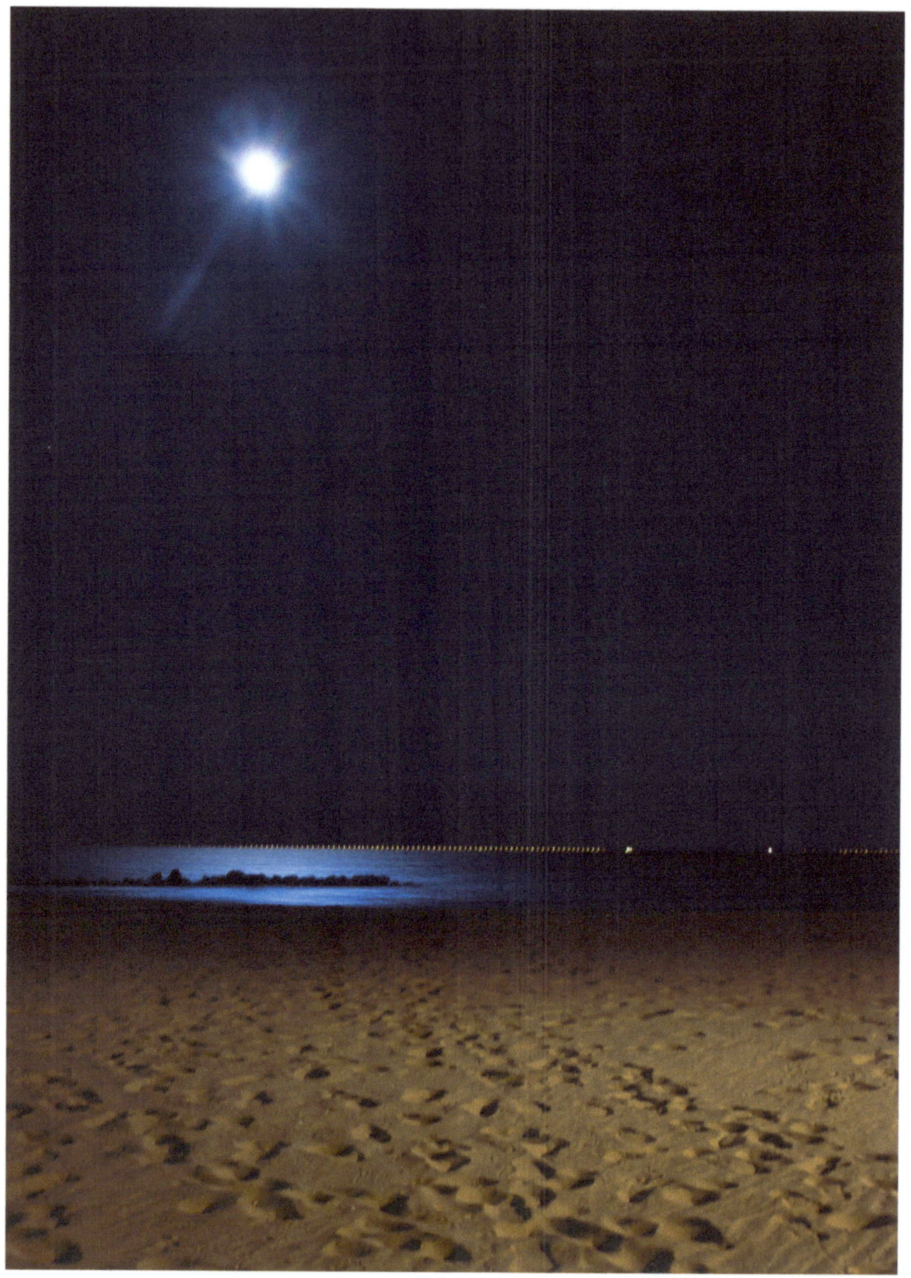

The blue hour at Buckroe Beach, Hampton, Virginia.

Take head shots in portrait orientation so there is less background.

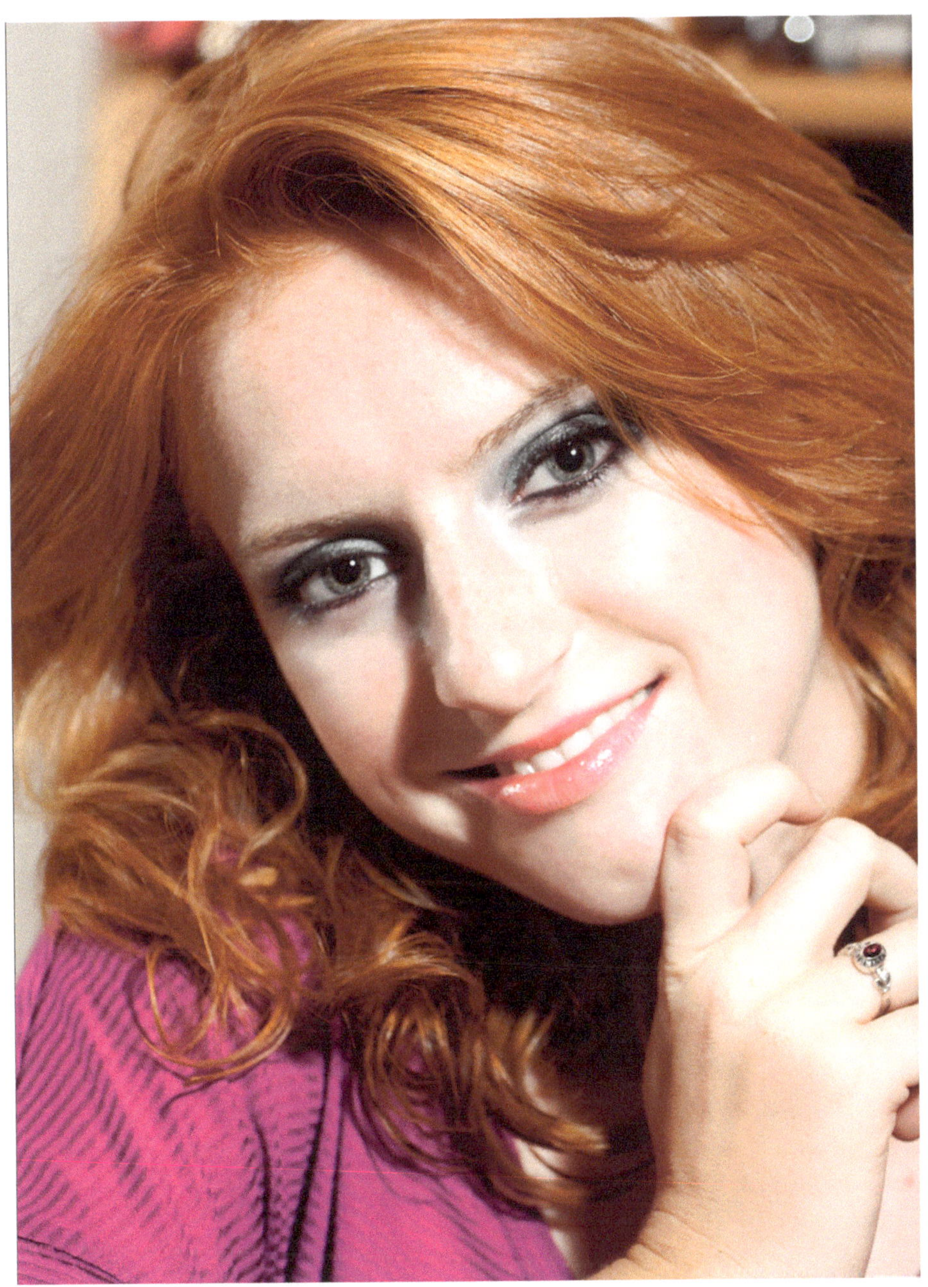

A close up portrait of Rachel.

You can still include some background in portrait shots.

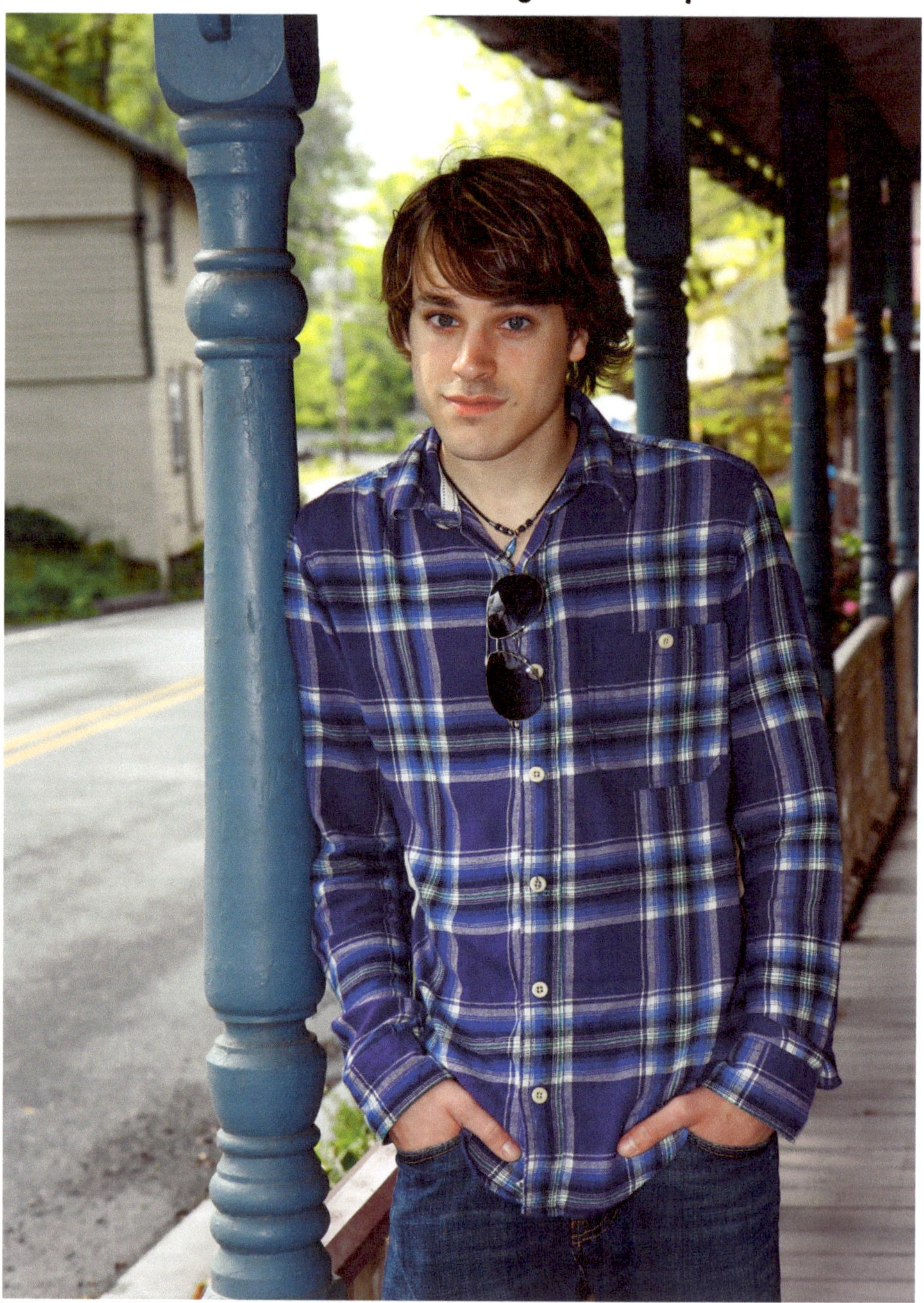

Cody's high school photo session.

Landscape orientation is side to side. It's great for scenic shots.

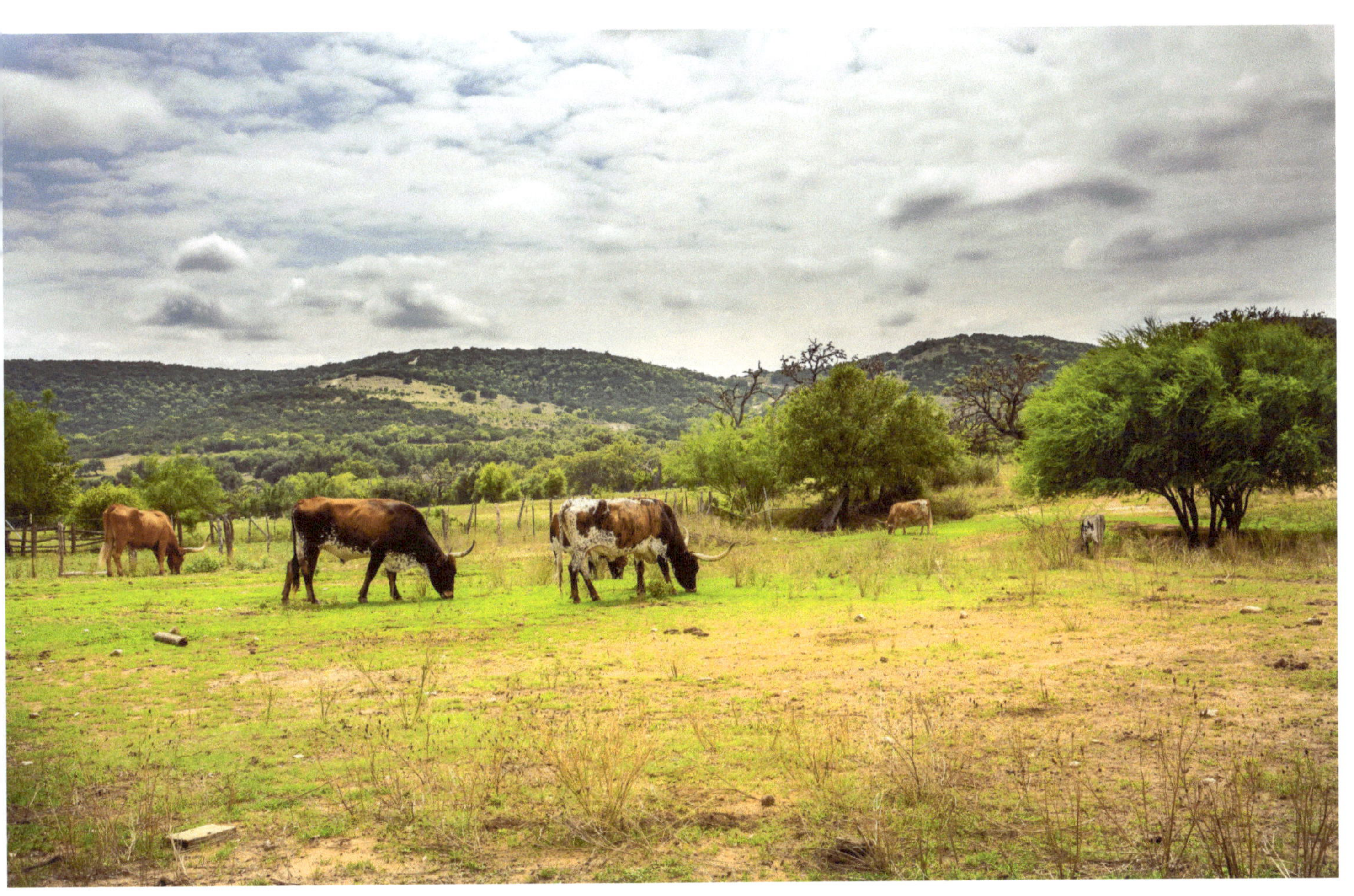

Longhorn cattle at Dixie Dude Ranch in Bandera, Texas.

Including more background helps tell the more of the story.

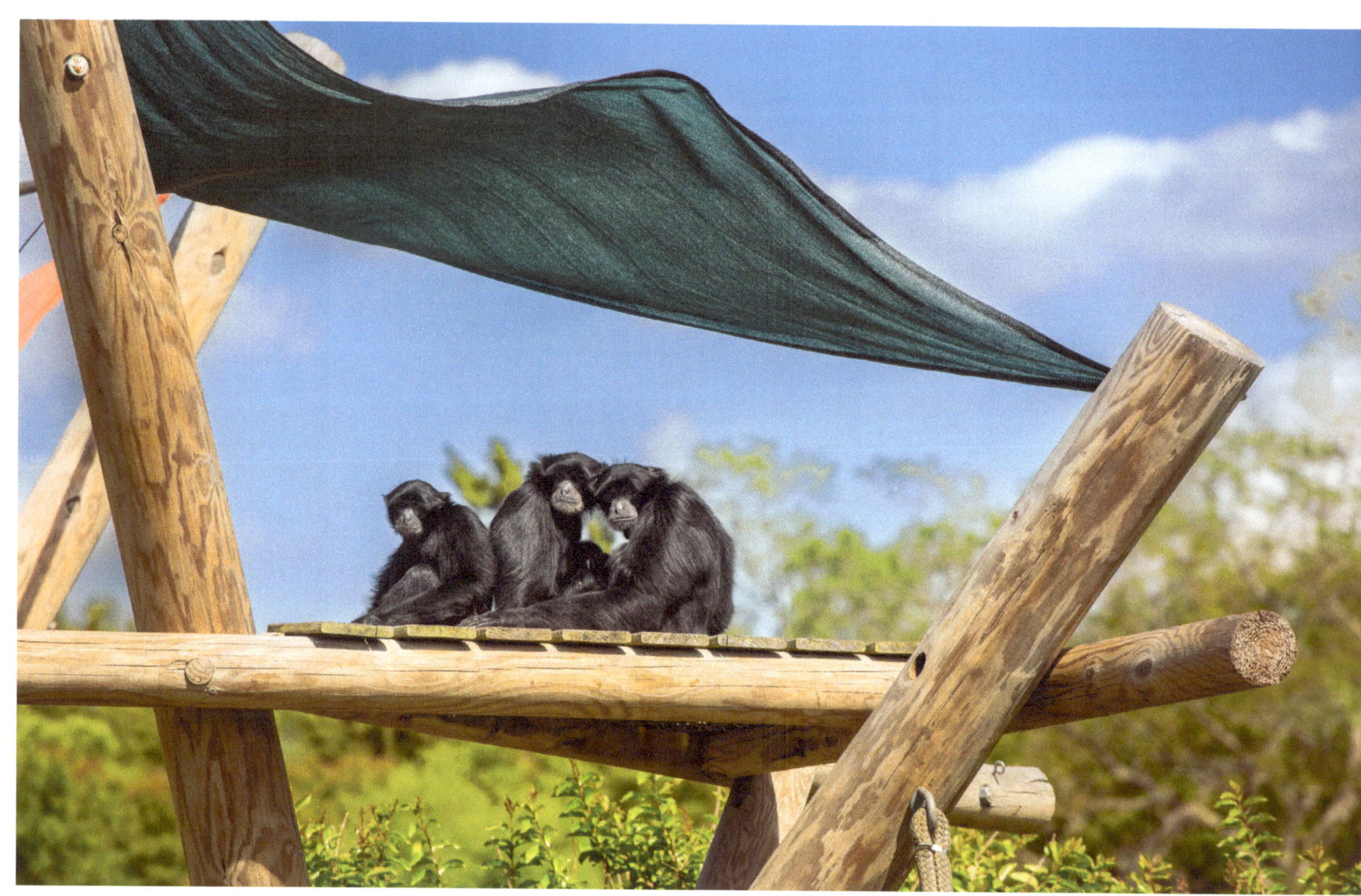

The Virginia Zoo, Norfolk, Virginia.

Zoomed in, it's hard to tell if they are in the zoo or in the wild.

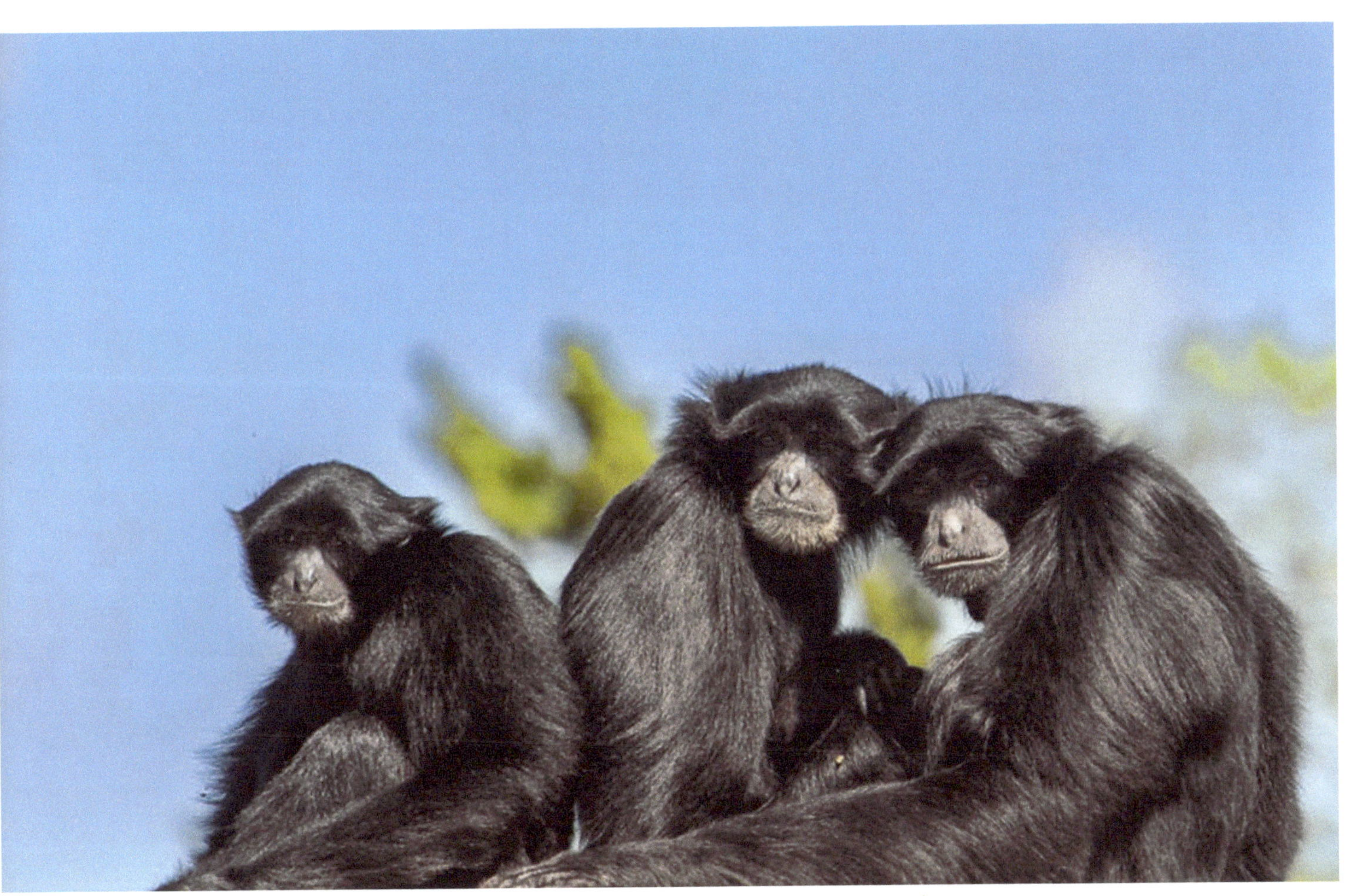

Zoos are great places to get animal photos.

A field of leaves might be a boring photo.

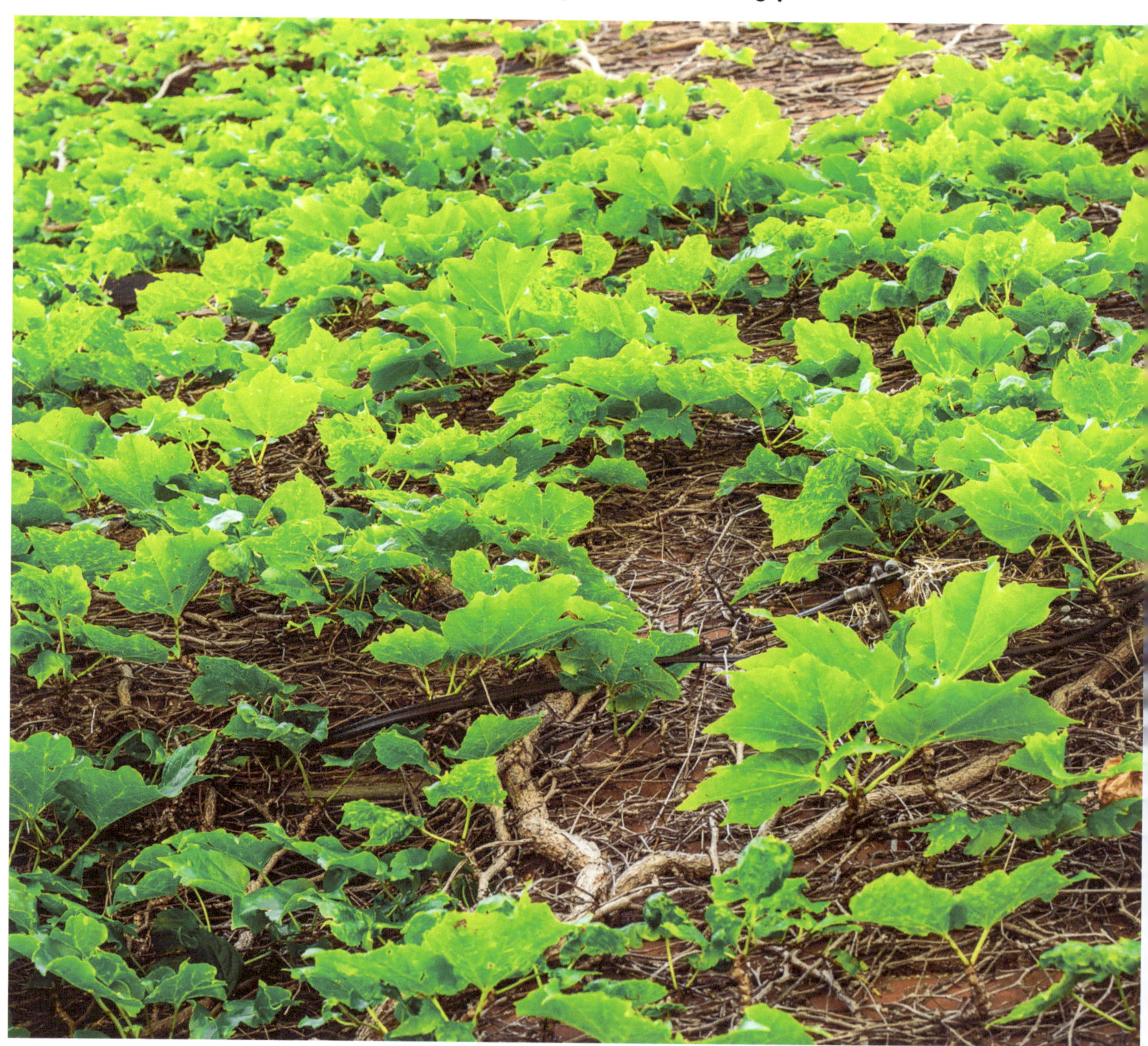

These vines covered my neighbor's yard.

But when you get closer, it's like another world.

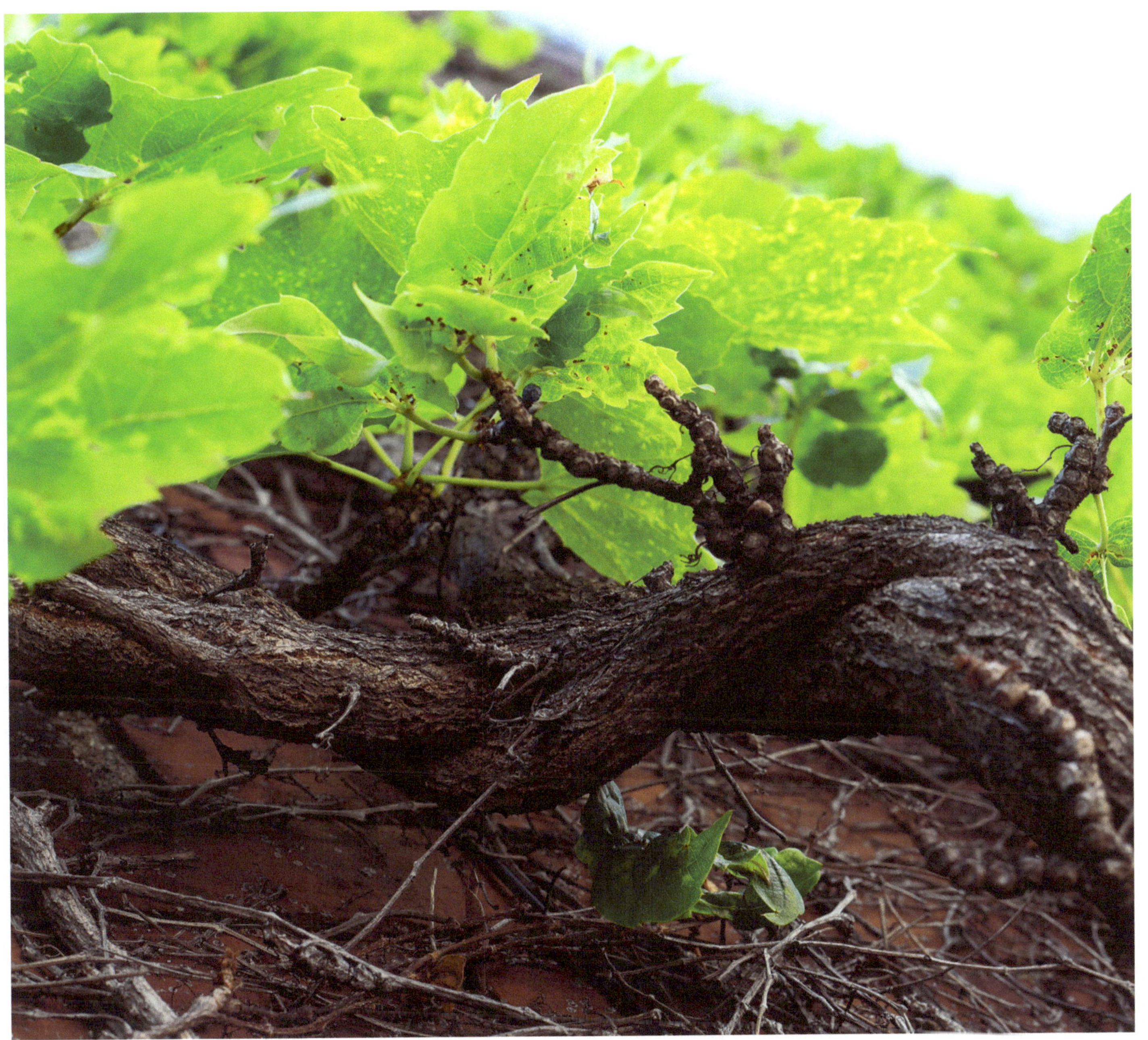

Can you imagine fairies living here?

Camera

Most of the images in this book were taken with a professional DSLR (Digital Single Lens Reflex) camera. However, you can use all these techniques with a cell phone. A photographer friend once told me, "The best camera is the one you got."

This photo of Jazzy was taken with my cell phone and it's one of my favorites.

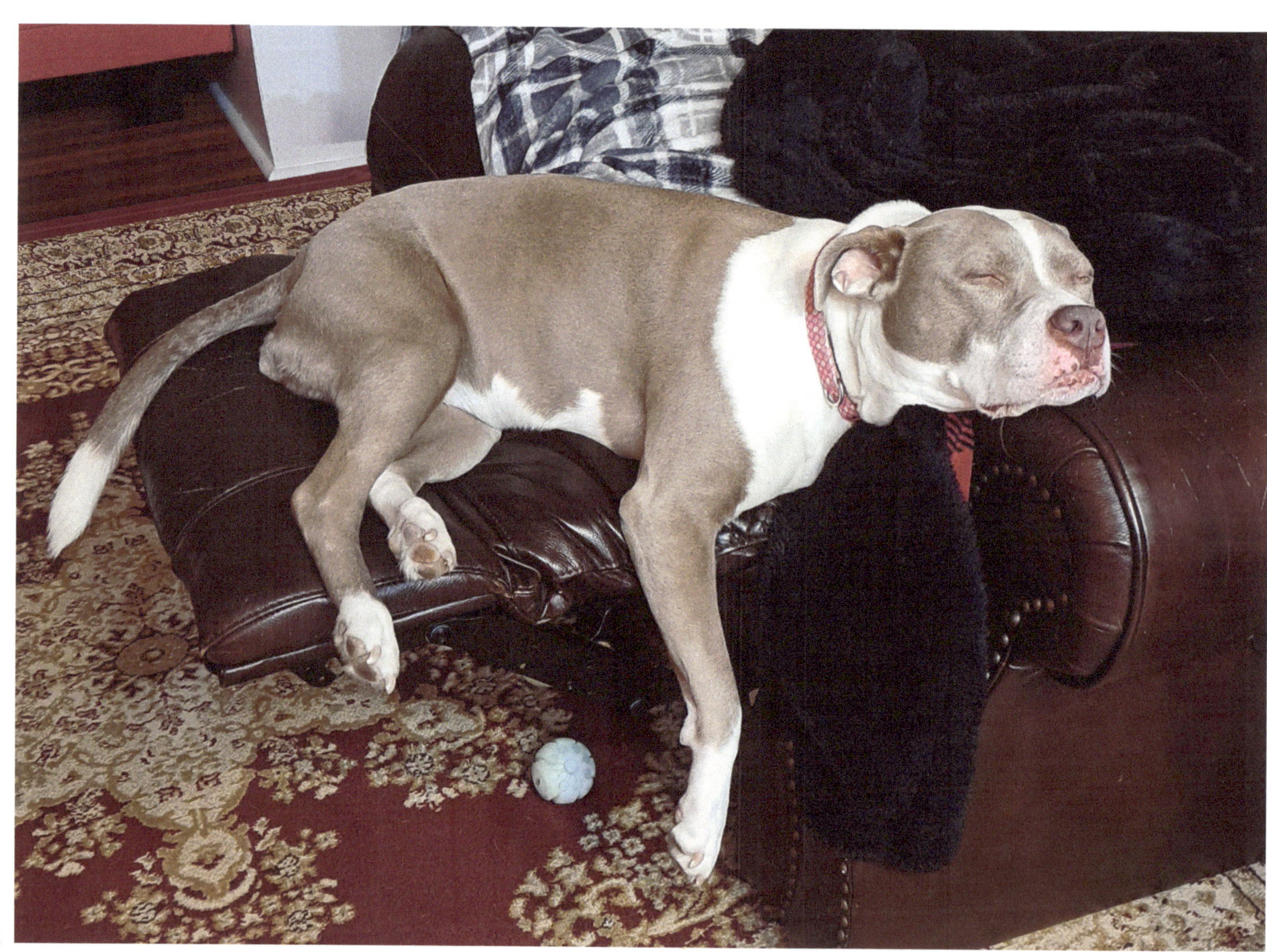

Composition

Composition: What a photographer includes in each picture. Where is the subject? How do you use the light. From what angle do you take the picture? Will you blur any part of it? Composition is up to personal taste, but for beginning photographers, using the Rule of Thirds is a good start to learning.

The Rule of Thirds

Imagine taking a picture and drawing a tic-tac-toe over it. By putting the subject of your photo near one of the intersecting lines, the image will seem to be better than if the subject is in the middle. This is a general rule that can be broken, but if you are just learning photography, it will help guide you to better composition.

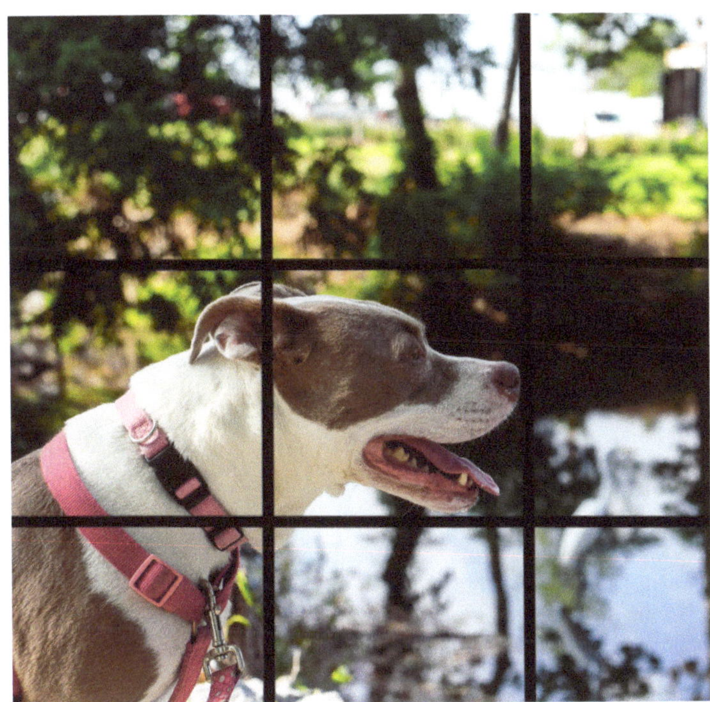
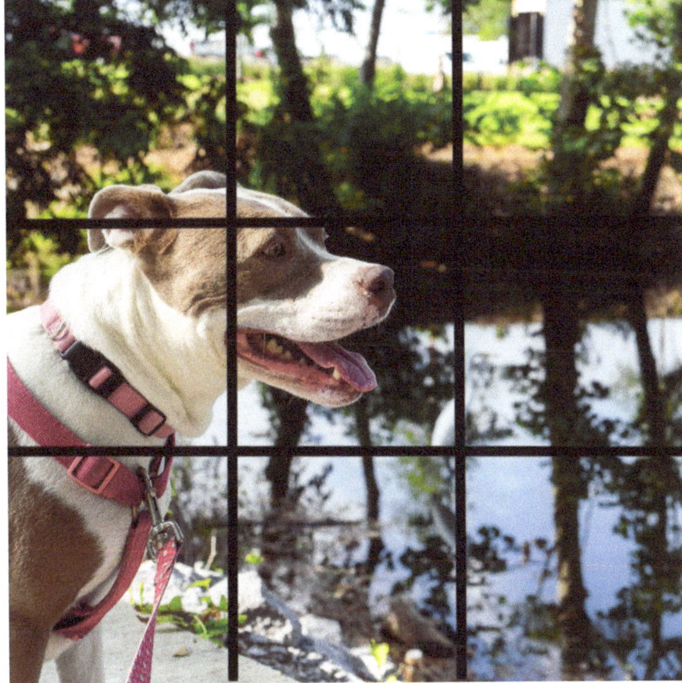

Light and Shadows

This book shows you how light creates shadows and how it can be used to get rid of shadows. The sun is far away from us. On a clear day, the sun is a small, concentrated light source. Shadows will be dark and have hard edges.

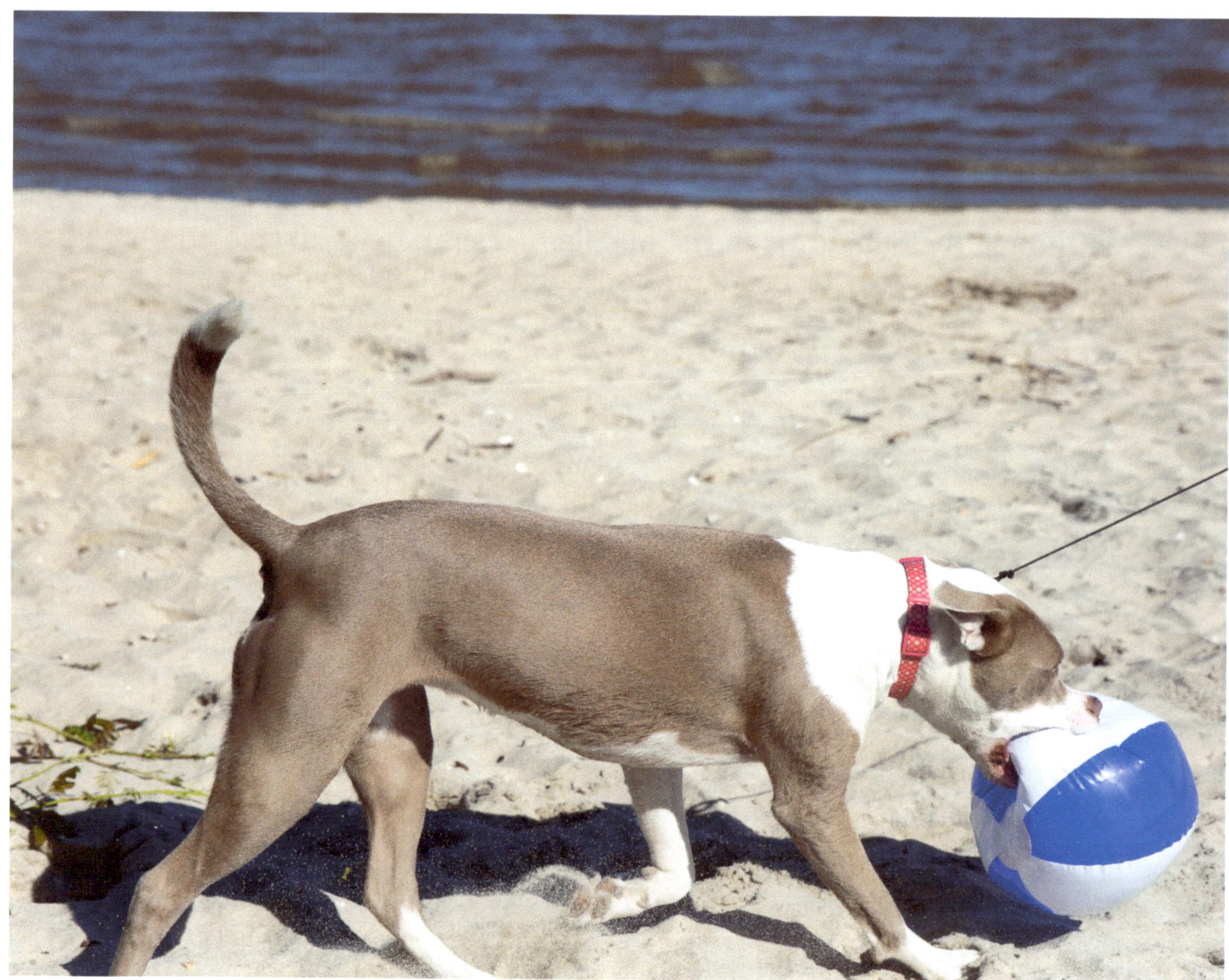

But with clouds in the sky, or using trees for shade, the light is sprinkled all over which makes it softer. Photographers have other tools to help them soften the light from the sun or from their flashes.

In this picture, the sun was hidden by the rain clouds. You can barely see Jazzy's shadow.

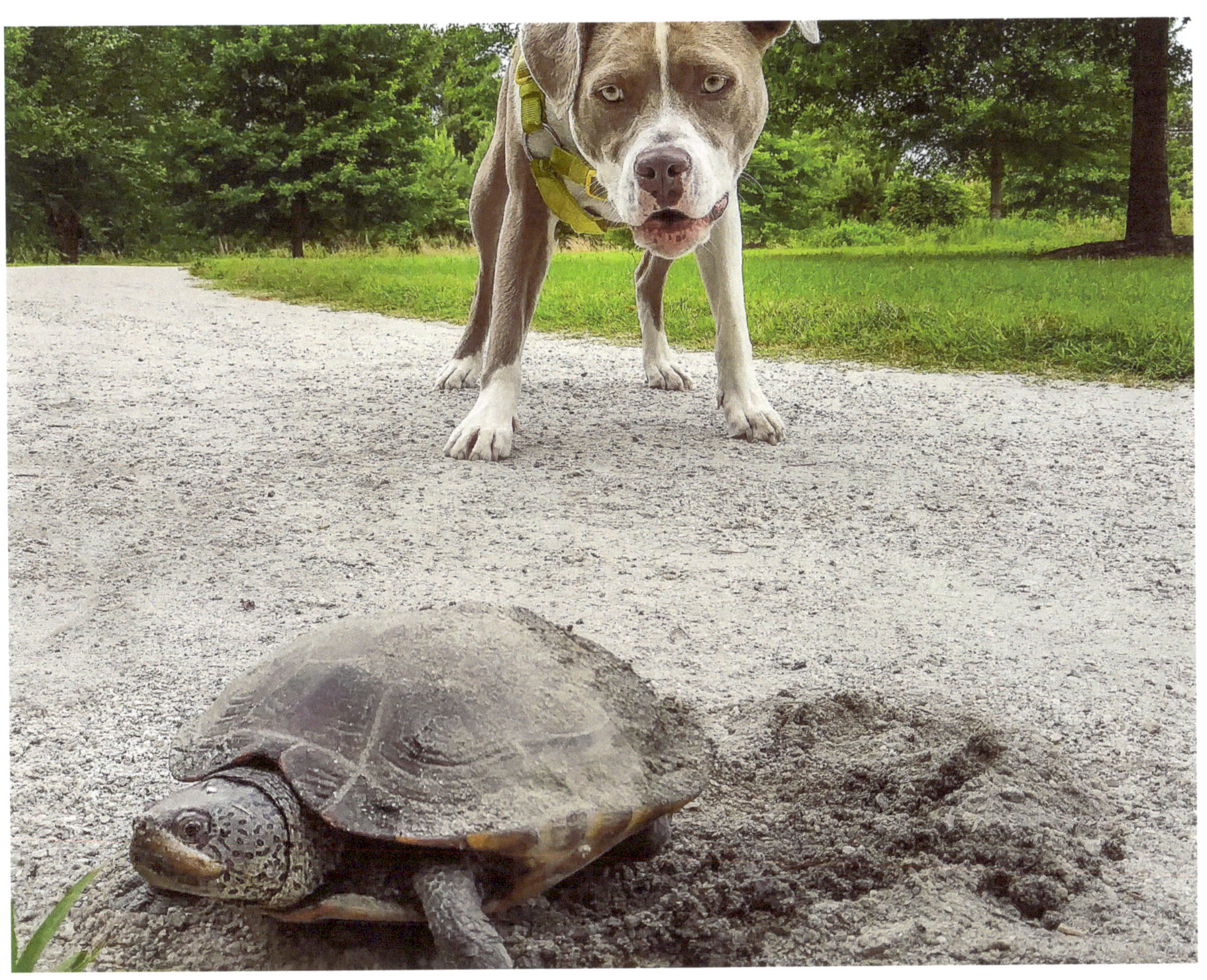

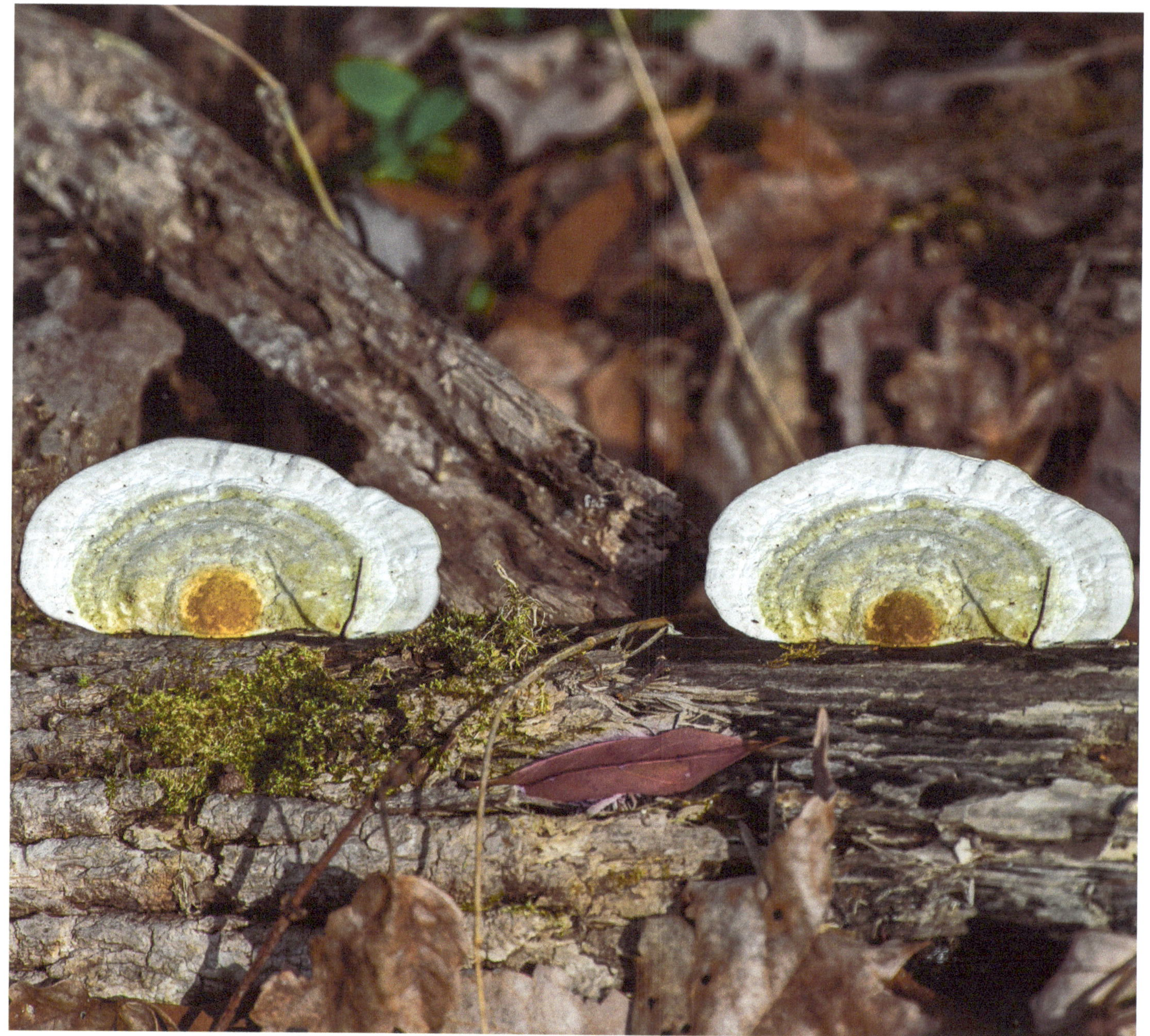

Mushrooms found on a fallen tree in Smithfield, Virginia.

If you like this book, please take a moment to review it, or my other books.

https://www.amazon.com/author/sonjamcgiboney

Sign up for my monthly newsletter!

It's full of stories, crafts, guest authors, and more.

https://www.jazzysbooks.com/

Other books that you might like!

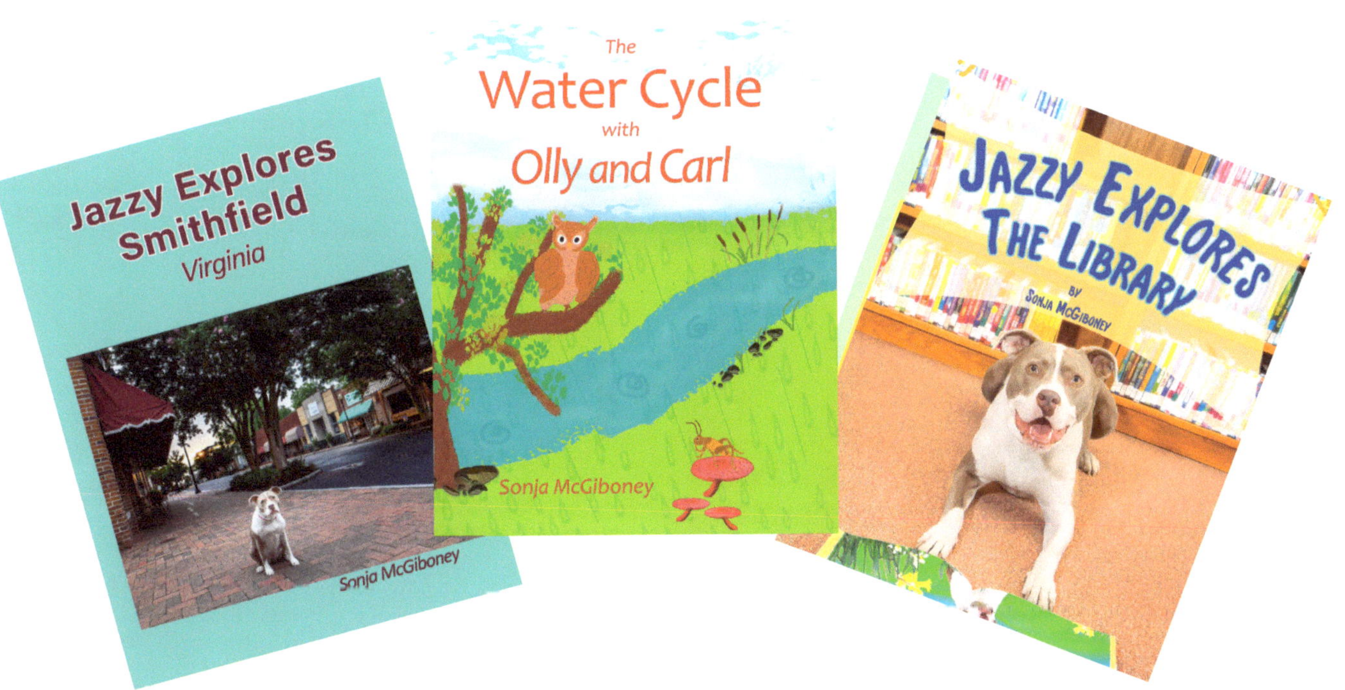

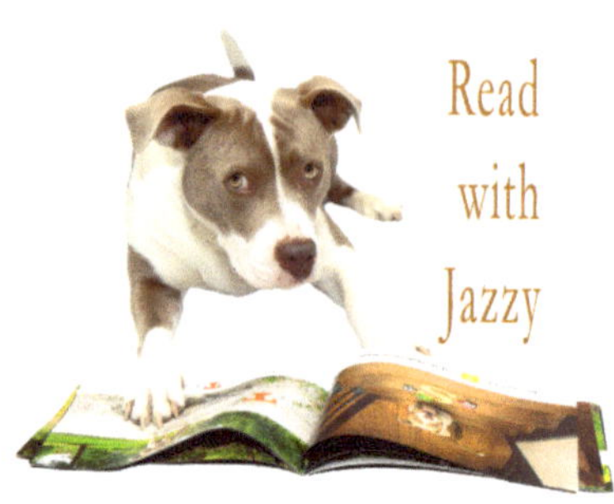

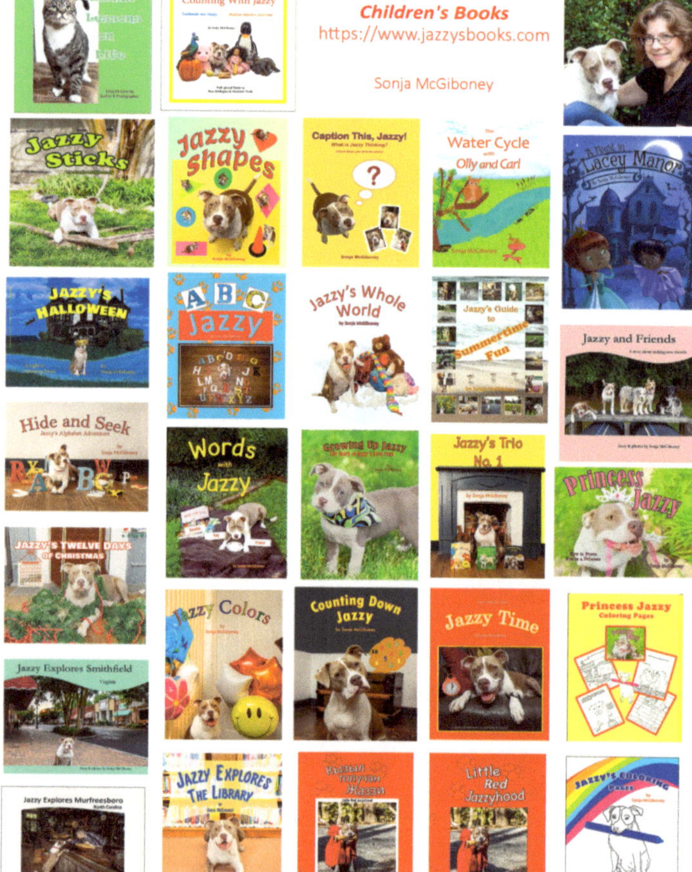

Sonja McGiboney creates children's books. Her *Jazzy's Books* series are full of beautiful photographs and are geared to help young children with concepts such as the alphabet, counting, friendship, shapes, and self-worth.

She is happy to share that her first chapter book, *A Night in Lacey Manor*, launched in March, 2025.

In her spare time, Sonja teaches piano, is learning to play the violin, enjoys photographing animals, and taking long car trips to photograph scenic roads in the U.S.

www.ingramcontent.com/pod-product-compliance
Lightning Source LLC
Chambersburg PA
CBHW042202030726
47602CB00007B/100